Editor-in-Chief and Founder:
  Lyndon H. LaRouche, Jr.
Editorial Board: *Lyndon H. LaRouche, Jr. , Helga
  Zepp-LaRouche, Robert Ingraham, Tony
  Papert, Gerald Rose, Dennis Small, Jeffrey
  Steinberg, William Wertz*
Co-Editors: *Robert Ingraham, Tony Papert*
Technology: *Marsha Freeman*
Books: *Katherine Notley*
Ebooks: *Richard Burden*
Graphics: *Alan Yue*
Photos: *Stuart Lewis*
Circulation Manager: *Stanley Ezrol*

INTELLIGENCE DIRECTORS
Counterintelligence: *Jeffrey Steinberg, Michele
  Steinberg*
Economics: *John Hoefle, Marcia Merry Baker,
  Paul Gallagher*
History: *Anton Chaitkin*
Ibero-America: *Dennis Small*
Russia and Eastern Europe: *Rachel Douglas*
United States: *Debra Freeman*

INTERNATIONAL BUREAUS
Bogotá: *Miriam Redondo*
Berlin: *Rainer Apel*
Copenhagen: *Tom Gillesberg*
Houston: *Harley Schlanger*
Lima: *Sara Madueño*
Melbourne: *Robert Barwick*
Mexico City: *Gerardo Castilleja Chávez*
New Delhi: *Ramtanu Maitra*
Paris: *Christine Bierre*
Stockholm: *Ulf Sandmark*
United Nations, N.Y.C.: *Leni Rubinstein*
Washington, D.C.: *William Jones*
Wiesbaden: *Göran Haglund*

ON THE WEB
e-mail: eirns@larouchepub.com
www.larouchepub.com
www.executiveintelligencereview.com
www.larouchepub.com/eiw
Webmaster: *John Sigerson*
Assistant Webmaster: *George Hollis*
Editor, Arabic-language edition: *Hussein Askary*

EIR (ISSN 0273-6314) *is published weekly
(50 issues), by EIR News Service, Inc.,
P.O. Box 17390, Washington, D.C. 20041-0390.
(703) 297-8434*

European Headquarters: E.I.R. GmbH, Postfach
Bahnstrasse 9a, D-65205, Wiesbaden, Germany
Tel: 49-611-73650
Homepage: http://www.eir.de
e-mail: info@eir.de
Director: Georg Neudecker

Montreal, Canada: 514-461-1557
eir@eircanada.ca

Denmark: EIR - Danmark, Sankt Knuds Vej 11,
basement left, DK-1903 Frederiksberg, Denmark.
Tel.: +45 35 43 60 40, Fax: +45 35 43 87 57. e-mail:
eirdk@hotmail.com.

Mexico City: EIR, Sor Juana Inés de la Cruz 242-2
Col. Agricultura C.P. 11360
Delegación M. Hidalgo, México D.F.
Tel. (5525) 5318-2301
eirmexico@gmail.com

Copyright: ©2017 EIR News Service. All rights
reserved. Reproduction in whole or in part without
permission strictly prohibited.

Canada Post Publication Sales Agreement
#40683579

Postmaster: Send all address changes to *EIR*, P.O.
Box 17390, Washington, D.C. 20041-0390.

Signed articles in *EIR* represent the views of the authors,
and not necessarily those of the Editorial Board.

I0839697

Another Hoax from Christopher Steele

EIR Contents

www.larouchepub.com   Volume 45, Number 12, March 23, 2018

Wochit News

ANOTHER HOAX FROM CHRISTOPHER STEELE

Skripal Poisoning a Desperate British Attempt to Resurrect Their American Coup

by Barbara Boyd

March 18—In this report, we will explore the strategic significance of major events in the world starting in February 2018. Our goal is to precisely situate British Prime Minister Theresa May's March 12-14 mad effort to manufacture a new "weapons of mass destruction" hoax based on the alleged Skripal poisoning, using the same people (the MI6 intelligence grouping around Sir Richard Dearlove) and script (an intelligence fraud concerning weapons of mass destruction) which were used to draw the United States into the disastrous Iraq War.

The Skripal poisoning fraud also directly involves British agent Christopher Steele, the central figure in the ongoing coup against Donald Trump. This time the British information warfare operation is aimed at directly provoking Russia, while maintaining the targeting of the U.S. population and President Trump.

As the fevered, war-like media coverage and hysteria surrounding the case make clear, a certain section of the British elite seems prepared to risk everything on behalf of its dying imperial system. Despite the hype, economic warfare and sanctions appear to be the British weapons of choice—Vladimir Putin, as we shall see, recently called the West's nuclear bluff. With the British "Russiagate" coup against Donald Trump fizzling, exposing British agent Christopher Steele and a slew of his American friends to criminal prosecution, a new tool was desperately needed to back the President of the United States into the British geopolitical corner shared by most of the American establishment. The tool they are using to do this is an intelligence hoax, a tried-and-true British product.

According to the British spy tale, a former Russian military intelligence colonel, Sergei Skripal, who spied for Great Britain in Russia from the early 1990s until 2004, was poisoned, along with his daughter, on March 4 in Salisbury, England, using a nerve agent "of a type developed by Russia." In 2010, Skripal had been exchanged in a spy swap between the United States and Russia. He had served six years in a Russian prison for spying for Britain. He had been living in the open in Britain for the last eight years. Skripal's MI6 recruiter and handler, Pablo Miller, listed himself as a consultant

Theresa May's full statement on Russian spy's poisoning

By James Masters, CNN
Updated 9:14 AM ET, Tue March 13, 2018

British Prime Minister Theresa May speaking to the Parliament.

to Orbis Business Intelligence, Christopher Steele's British company, on his LinkedIn profile. When the London *Daily Telegraph* called attention to the Orbis reference, it was removed from the profile. Steele, who worked on the Trump dossier through his company Orbis, has denied that Miller worked directly on that dossier.

Theresa May and her foreign minister, Boris Johnson, insist there is only one person who could be responsible for the poisoning—described as an act of war—and that person is Vladimir Putin. No evidence has been offered to support this claim. No plausible motive has been provided as to why Putin would order such a provocative murder now, ahead of the World Cup, when the Russiagate coup in the United States has lost all momentum. Rather than following the protocols of the Organization for the Prohibition of Chemical Weapons (OPCW), which require that evidence of the alleged agent be presented to Russia, the eccentric and unpopular May instead delivered an ultimatum to Russia, and whipped up war fever throughout the UK. She now seeks to pull Donald Trump and NATO into ever more aggressive moves against Russia.

Thus, as with Christopher Steele's dirty dossier against Donald Trump, the British claims against Putin are an evidence-free exercise of raw power. The Anglo-American establishment instructs us: "trust this, ignore the stinky factless content presented in this dossier—just note that it is backed by very important intelligence agencies which could cook your goose if you object."

A short statement of the reasons why the British are now staging the Skripal provocation can be found in a March 14 London *Daily Telegraph* call to arms by Allister Heath, who rants: "We need a new world order to take on totalitarian capitalists in Russia and China. Such an alliance would dramatically shift the global balance of power, and allow the liberal democracies fi-

nally to fight back. It would endow the world with the sorts of robust institutions that are required to contain Russia and China. Britain needs a new role in the world; building such a network would be our perfect mission." Across the pond, as they say, a similar foundational statement was made by 68 former Obama Administration officials who have formed a group called National Security Action, aimed at securing Trump's impeachment and attacking Russia and China.

Russia and China have embarked on a massive infrastructure building project in Eurasia, the center of all British geopolitical fantasies since the time of Halford Mackinder. China's "Belt and Road Initiative" now encompasses more than 140 nations in the largest infrastructure-building project ever undertaken in human history. This project is a true economic engine for the future. At the same time, the neo-liberal economies of the trans-Atlantic region continue to see their productive potentials sucked dry by the massive piles of debt they have created since the 2008 financial collapse. This debt is now on a hair trigger for implosion. It is estimated by banking insiders that the City of London is sitting on a derivatives powderkeg of $700 trillion, with over-the-counter derivatives accounting for another $570 trillion. The City of London will bear the major impact of the coming derivatives collapse.

In this strategic geometry, President Trump's support for peaceful collaboration with Russia during the campaign, and his personal friendship with China's President Xi Jinping, have marked him for the relentless coup-drive waged by the British and their U.S. friends.

On top of that, President Putin delivered a mammoth strategic shock on March 1, showing new Russian weapons systems based on new physical principles, which render present U.S. ABM systems and much of current U.S. war-fighting doctrine obsolete, together with the vaunted first strike capacity with which NATO has surrounded Russia. Not only is the West sitting on a new financial collapse, its vaunted military superiority has just been flanked.

It is very clear that a strategic choice now confronts the human race. In 1984, Lyndon LaRouche wrote a very profound document, "Draft Memorandum of Agreement Between the U.S. and the U.S.S.R." In it, he developed the concrete basis for peace between the two superpowers at the moment when the United States had adopted the LaRouche/Reagan doctrine of strategic defense. Both Reagan and LaRouche had proposed

The British Empire Is Finished

by Rachel Brown

March 18—Though it may seem to some credulous readers of the *New York Times* that Great Britain is in a position of moral authority and power in its recent accusations against Russia, the opposite is the truth. In reality, the British Empire is in a last-ditch effort to try to save its crumbling system. Teresa May's ridiculous cries are indications of the desperation of London, and reminiscent of the threats often heard emerging from dying empires. The fact that the Skripal poisoning occurred only three days after President Putin's historically momentous speech should not be overlooked. Putin announced a new series of advanced weapons that render the Obama encirclement of Russia impotent.

The fragility of the case is indicative of its political necessity. Not only is there no content to the allegations of Russia's role in the Skripal attack—no samples having been provided as required under the OPCW protocols—the facts of the case point again to the circles of Christopher Steele, the British MI6 agent and author of the now discredited "Golden Shower" dossier, which was at the center of claims of Trump campaign ties to Russia. Sergei Skripal, a colonel in Russian military intelligence, was recruited to work for British intelligence by MI6 agent Pablo Miller while Steele was an undercover MI6 agent stationed in Moscow. After being caught and sentenced to 18 years in prison for treason, Skripal was let out as part of a prisoner exchange and moved to the UK. He again befriended Pablo Miller while Miller worked for Orbis, Christopher Steele's company, during the period the Steele dossier was being written.

Now the Russiagate case against President Trump is falling apart in the United States. The House Intelligence Committee concluded there was no Russian collusion, and FBI Deputy Director Andrew McCabe was fired. Christopher Steele has been referred to the U.S. Justice Department for criminal prosecution, and is defending himself from lawsuits in the UK and U.S.A. At a recent hearing in London, none other than representatives of the British Foreign Office showed up to demonstrate the concern of the British government for this allegedly "private" citizen.

Meanwhile, the potential of a Korean peace agreement is a very real prospect, while more and more countries are joining China's New Silk Road. Eleven European Union nations have signed cooperation documents with the Chinese government, and 13,673 trips were made by China-Europe express freight trains in 2017, more than in the previous six years combined. Greece's Port of Piraeus has again become one of the largest in Europe, helping that financially distressed country to improve its economic condition. French President Emmanuel Macron declared during a recent visit to China that France is joining the New Silk Road, while South American and Caribbean nations are openly expressing their intent to join as well.

The London-directed trans-Atlantic establishment is beyond desperate. This is why we are seeing the British themselves—in the person of Prime Minister May—taking the point on this. This public exposure of their own guiding hand is not something the Brits like. They are flailing, and attempting to throw monkey wrenches everywhere: in Syria, with North Korea, in the Ukraine, and other conflicts they have generated—anything to keep their grasp on world power just a little bit longer. The time could not be more urgent to act on the truth—the British empire is finished, and the United States must eliminate the British-run coup and join the New Silk Road paradigm for a lasting peace.

President Putin addressing the Federal Assembly, March 1, 2018.

China President Xi Jinping speaks to the Party Congress in October 2017.

that the Russians and the United States cooperate in building and developing strategic defense against offensive nuclear weapons, based on new physical principles, thereby eliminating the threat of nuclear annihilation.

According to the LaRouche Doctrine, "The political foundation for durable peace must be: a) the unconditional sovereignty of each and all nation states, and b) cooperation among sovereign states to the effect of promoting unlimited opportunities to participate in the benefits of technological progress, to the mutual benefit of each and all."

Both China, in President Xi's October Address to the Party Congress, and Russia, in Putin's March 1 address to the Federal Assembly, have set a course to produce technological progress capable of being shared in by all. They both outline major infrastructure projects and dedicating massive funding to exploring the frontiers of science, technology, and space exploration. Donald Trump, in both his campaign and his presidency, has embraced similar views. The British and their American friends, however, are devotees of a completely different and failing economic system, a system soundly rejected in Brexit, in the election of Donald Trump, and most recently in the Italian elections.

Just look at the events of February and March from this standpoint. It is no accident that Christopher Steele turns up, smack dab in the middle of the Skripal poisoning hoax.

Exposure of British as U.S. Election Meddlers Weakens Anti-Trump Coup

On Feb. 2, the House Permanent Select Committee on Intelligence released a memo demonstrating that the Obama Justice Department and FBI committed an outright fraud on the FISA court in obtaining surveillance warrants on Carter Page, a volunteer for Donald Trump's 2016 presidential campaign. The bogus warrant applications relied heavily on the dirty British dossier authored by MI6's "former" Russian intelligence chief, Christopher Steele, who had been paid by Hillary Clinton's campaign and the Democratic National Committee to paint Donald Trump as a Manchurian candidate—as a pawn of Russian President Vladimir Putin.

According to the House Intelligence memo and other aspects of its investigation, Steele confided to Bruce Ohr, a high official in the DOJ, that he, Steele, hated Trump with a passion and would do "anything" to prevent Trump's election. Steele was using the fact of an FBI investigation of his allegations as part of a "full spectrum" British information warfare campaign conducted against candidate Trump with the full complicity of Obama's intelligence chiefs. (See Peter Van Buren, "Christopher Steele: The Real Foreign Influence in the 2016 U.S. Election?" *The American Conservative*, February 15, 2018.) None of the true facts about the actual motive for, and sponsors of, the DOJ applications involving Carter Page were revealed to the FISA Court in the filings made by former Deputy Attorney General Sally Yates, former FBI Director James

White House/Pete Souza

Obama's former Deputy National Security Adviser John Brennan.

LBJ Library/Jay Godwin

Obama's Director of National Intelligence, James Clapper.

cc/Rich Girard

Former FBI Director James Comey.

Comey, or current Deputy Attorney General Rod Rosenstein.

The House Intelligence Committee memo was quickly followed by a declassified letter on Feb. 5, in which Senators Chuck Grassley and Lindsay Graham referred Christopher Steele to the Department of Justice (DOJ) for criminal prosecution, based on false statements he made to the FBI about his contacts with the news media. No doubt the criminal referral sent chills down the spines not only of Christopher Steele and his British colleagues, but also of those former Obama officials conspiring against Trump.

In the same week, House Intelligence Chairman Devin Nunes announced that he would be conducting investigations into the role of the Obama State Department and intelligence chiefs in the circulation and use of Christopher Steele's dirty dossier. These investigations have been widely reported to focus on John Brennan and James Clapper—Brennan for widely promoting the dirty British work product, and Clapper for leaks associated with *BuzzFeed*'s publication and legitimization of the dirty British work product. Remind yourself every time you hear media explosions against Trump by either Clapper (congressional perjurer and proponent of the theory that the Russians are genetically predisposed to

Christopher Steele's lawyers say he shouldn't be forced to testify

Lawyers say that a lengthy questioning would amount to a 'fishing' expedition

screw the United States) or Brennan (gopher for George Tenet's perpetual war and torture regime and Grand Inquisitor for Barack Obama's serial assassinations by baseball card). They are next in the barrel, so to speak.

The January 11, 2017 *BuzzFeed* publication of the Steele dossier was meant to permanently poison Trump's incoming administration, and is the subject of libel suits both in Florida and London. In the London case, the British are ready to invoke the Official Secrets Act to protect Christopher Steele. In the Florida case, Steele has been ordered to sit for deposition despite numerous delays and stalling tactics.

The Congressional investigation of the State Department is focused on John Kerry, Kerry's aide Jonathan Winer, Victoria Nuland, and Clinton operative Cody Shearer. Nuland utilized Christopher Steele as a primary intelligence source while running the U.S. regime change operations in Ukraine in alliance with neo-Nazis. She greenlighted Steele's initial meetings with the FBI about Donald Trump. Winer deployed himself to vouch for Steele to various news publications collaborating with British agent Steele and his U.S. employer, Fusion GPS, in Steele's media warfare operations against Trump.

On March 12, the House Intelligence Committee

Obama's Secretary of State John Kerry (left) and Jonathan Winer.

Obama's Assistant Secretary of State, Victoria Nuland.

announced that it had completed its Russia investigation. It stated that it found *"no collusion, coordination, or conspiracy between the Trump campaign and Russia."* Its draft final report was to have been provided to the Democrats on the Committee on March 13 for comment and then submitted to declassification review.

On March 15, four U.S. Senators from the Senate Judiciary Committee, Chuck Grassley, Lindsey Graham, John Cornyn, and Thom Tillis, called for the appointment of a Special Counsel to investigate the DOJ and FBI with respect to the Russiagate investigation. They particularly focused on the use of the Steele dossier, FISA abuse, the disclosure of classified information to the press, and the criminal investigation and case of former Trump National Security Advisor Michael Flynn. Separately, House Oversight Chairman Trey Gowdy and House Judiciary Chairman Bob Goodlatte have asked the Justice Department to appoint a Special Counsel on similar grounds.

On March 16, James Comey's Deputy FBI Director, Andrew McCabe, was fired as the result of recommendations by the FBI's Office of Professional Responsibility (OPR). The OPR recommendation resulted from Justice Department Inspector General Michael Horowitz's investigation

FBI

Andrew McCabe

of McCabe's actions with respect to the Clinton email investigation and the Clinton Foundation. McCabe claimed that this was part of a plot against himself, Comey, and Special Counsel Robert Mueller. Michael Horowitz, however, is an actual Washington straight shooter appointed to his post by Barack Obama. The OPR is the FBI's own disciplinary agency. Horowitz's report is expected to be extremely critical of McCabe, citing a "lack of candor" (i.e., lying) with respect to the investigation. Whatever the corrupt media might claim, the facts here have been thoroughly investigated by McCabe's former FBI subordinates. They think his lies and other actions disgrace the FBI and don't entitle him to a pension.

Horowitz's report on the Clinton investigations—which have already unearthed the texts between former Russiagate lead case agent Peter Strzok and his mistress, FBI lawyer Lisa Page, proclaiming their hatred of Donald Trump and the need for an "insurance policy" against his election—is expected to be released very soon. According to the House Intelligence Committee, the Strzok/Page texts also reveal that Strzok was a close friend of U.S. District Court Judge Rudolph Contreras. Contreras sits on the FISA court, took Michael Flynn's guilty plea, and then promptly recused himself from Michael Flynn's case for reasons which remain undisclosed.

Despite its exoneration of the President and thorough discrediting of the British Steele operation, the House Intelligence Committee dangerously accepts the myth that the Russians hacked the Democratic National Committee, the Democratic Congressional Campaign Committee, and the emails of Clinton Campaign Chairman John Podesta, and then provided the hacked information to WikiLeaks for publication. Its final report states, however, that Putin's intervention was not in support of Donald Trump, as previously claimed by Obama's intelligence chiefs. The Senators seeking a new Special Counsel also salute this dangerous fraud.

As we have previously reported, the myth that Putin hacked the Democrats and provided the hacked emails to WikiLeaks, has been substantively refuted by the investigations of the Veteran Intelligence Professionals for Sanity (VIPS). In summary, the evidence points to a leak rather than a hack in the case of the DNC. Further, the NSA would have the evidence of any such hack or hacks, according to former NSA technical director Bill Binney, and would have provided it, even if in a classified setting. It is clear that the NSA has no such evidence. It is also clear that the United States and the British have cyber warfare capabilities fully capable of creating "false flag" cyber war incidents.

North Korea Talks Planned, While Russia and China Continue to Create the Conditions for a New Human Renaissance

In addition to the fizzling of the coup, the Western elites suffered through February and March for additional reasons. To the shock of the entire, smug Davos crowd, Donald Trump, working with Russia, China, and South Korea, appears to have gotten Kim Jong-un to the negotiating table concerning denuclearization of the Korean peninsula. Substantive talks have been scheduled for May. The breakthrough was announced by President Trump and South Korea on March 8.

On March 1, President Putin gave his historic two-hour address to the Russian Federal Assembly and the Russian people. Like President Xi's address to the Chinese Party Congress in October 2017, Putin focused on the goal of deeply reducing poverty in Russian society. Xi vowed in October to eliminate poverty from Chinese society altogether by 2020. In addition, Putin emphasized that Russia would undertake a huge city-building project across its vast rural frontiers and dramatically expand its modern infrastructure, including Russia's digital infrastructure. He put major emphasis on directing funds to basic scientific and technological progress. He emphasized that harnessing and stimulating the creative powers of individual human beings is the true driver of all economic progress.

China's Belt and Road Initiative also continued to advance. Great infrastructure projects are popping up throughout the world, including most specifically in Africa, which had been consigned to be a permanent, primitive looting-ground for Western interests. Among the recent breakthroughs is the great project to refill Lake Chad, a project known as "Transaqua," involving the Italian engineering firm Bonifica, the Chinese engineering and construction firm PowerChina, and the Lake Chad Basin Commission, which represents the African countries directly benefiting from the project. But the biggest strategic news of the last six weeks was contained in the last part of President Putin's speech. He showed various weapons, developed by Russian scientists in the wake of the U.S. abrogation of the ABM treaty and the Anglo-American campaign of color revolutions and NATO base-building in the former Soviet bloc. These weapons, based on new physical principles, render U.S. ABM defenses obsolete, together with many U.S. utopian war-fighting doctrines developed under the reigns of Obama and Bush. Putin emphasized that the economic and "defense" aspects of his speech were not separate. Rather, the scientific breakthroughs were based on an in-depth economic mobilization of the physical economy. He stressed that Russia's survival was dependent upon marshalling continuous creative breakthroughs in basic science and the high-technology spinoffs which result, and their propagation through the entire population. He stressed that such breakthroughs are the product of providing an actually human existence to the entire society.

Compare what Russia and China have set out to accomplish with respect to the physical economy of the Earth, with the second and third paragraphs of Lyndon LaRouche's prescription for a durable peace in the LaRouche Doctrine:

> The most crucial feature of present implementation of such a policy of durable peace is a profound change in the monetary, economic, and political relations between dominant powers and those relatively subordinated nations often classed as "developing nations." Unless the inequities lingering in the aftermath of modern colonialism are progressively remedied, there can be no durable peace on this planet.
>
> Insofar as the United States and the Soviet Union acknowledge the progress of the productive powers of labor throughout the planet to be in the vital strategic interests of each and both, the two powers are bound to that degree and in

that way by a common interest. This is the kernel of the political and economic policies of practice indispensable to the fostering of a durable peace between those two powers.

This is the perspective which has the British terrified and acting-out, insanely. Were Trump, Putin, and Xi to enter into negotiations based on the LaRouche Doctrine, a breakthrough will have occurred for all of mankind, a breakthrough to a permanent and durable peace. No neo-liberal, post-industrial, unipolar order can match this, no matter how much Allister Heath, Ms. May, or Boris Johnson rant and rave about it.

cc/Domusrulez

Sir Richard Dearlove, former head of MI6.

Christopher Steele's British Playground

As is well known by now, Christopher Steele was a long-time MI6 agent before "retiring" to form his own extremely lucrative private intelligence firm. The firm is said to have earned $200 million since its formation. Steele was an MI6 agent in Moscow around the time Skripal was recruited. He also later ran the MI6 Russia desk and would have known everything there was to know about Skripal. Pablo Miller, who recruited Skripal, worked for Steele's firm according to Miller's LinkedIn profile, and lived in the same town as Skripal.

Since Steele has been discredited in the United States, a huge fawning publicity campaign has been undertaken on his behalf. The campaign involves journalists who have collaborated directly with Steele in his smear job against Trump. Books by Luke Harding and Michael Isikoff seek to rebuild Steele's reputation. A fawning piece by Jane Mayer in the *New Yorker*, as implausible as it is long, has been foisted on the public for the same reason. There are some fascinating facts, however, in all this fawning prose:

• Steele described his business to Luke Harding as primarily providing research and reports to competing and feuding Russian oligarchs, many of whom use London as a base of operations. This is obviously a perfect cover for intelligence operations. It is also a very violent theater of operations. The oligarchs intersect both Western intelligence operations and Russian organized crime. They engage in deadly gang warfare.

• Steele and his partners are mentored by Sir Richard Dearlove, former head of MI6 and a critical player in the infamous "sexing up" and fabrication of the claim that Saddam Hussein had weapons of mass destruction, creating the rationale for the disastrous and genocidal Iraq War.

• Steele had been tasked to claim that Russia was interfering in Western elections during the entire post-Ukraine coup time-frame, when this black propaganda line began to be circulated widely. According to Jane Mayer's account, Steele called this "Project Charlemagne," and completed his report on it in April 2016, just before he undertook his hit job against Donald Trump. In his report, Steele claimed that Russia was interfering in the politics of France, Italy, the United Kingdom, Germany, and Turkey. He claimed that Russia was conducting social media warfare aimed at "inflaming fear and prejudice and had provided opaque financial support to favored politicians." He specifically targeted Silvio Berlusconi and Marine Le Pen. Steele also suggested that Russian aid was given to "lesser known right wing nationalists" in the United Kingdom and elsewhere, implying that the Russians were behind Brexit, with an overall goal of destroying the European Union.

Leaving aside Sergei Skripal's relationship with the central figure in the British-led coup against Donald Trump, it is clear that the May government's claim that he and his daughter were poisoned by a "novichok" nerve-agent, even if it is true, by no means makes a case that Putin's government was responsible. (It is of interest that as we were going to press on March 19, the foreign ministers of the European Union, after a briefing by British Foreign Secretary Boris Johnson that indicted Putin as responsible, issued a statement which condemned the poisoning of Skripal and his daughter, but pointedly failed to blame Putin or Russia.)

Craig Murray, a former British Ambassador to Uz-

Entrance to Porton Down, the oldest chemical warfare research lab in the world, established in 1916, according to The Guardian of London.

bekistan who maintains contacts in the Foreign and Commonwealth Office, wrote March 16 that Britain's chemical-warfare scientists at Porton Down, "are not able to identify the nerve agent as being of Russian manufacture, and have been resentful of the pressure being placed on them to do so. Porton Down would only sign up to the formulation of a type developed by Russia, after a rather difficult meeting where this was agreed as a compromise formulation. The Russians were allegedly researching, in the novichok program, a generation of nerve agents which could be produced from commercially available precursors such as insecticides and fertilizers. This substance is a novichok in that sense. It is of that type. Just as I am typing on a laptop of a type developed by the United States, though this one was made in China."

The background to Porton Down's reluctance, is of course former Prime Minister Blair's phony dossier on Iraqi WMD, which Lyndon LaRouche fought, alongside the late British arms expert David Kelly, who exposed the "dodgy dossier," at the time.

"To anybody with a Whitehall background this has been obvious for several days," Murray continues. "The government has never said the nerve agent was made in Russia, or that it can only be made in Russia. The exact formulation of a type developed by Russia was used by Theresa May in Parliament, used by the U.K. at the UN Security Council, used by Boris Johnson on the BBC yesterday and, most tellingly of all, 'of a type developed by Russia,' is the precise phrase used in the joint communique, issued by the U.K., U.S.A., France, and Germany yesterday."

The main account of the chemical weapons cited by Theresa May was written by a Soviet dissident chemist named Vil Mirzayanov who now lives in the United States and published a book about his work at the Soviets' Uzbekistan chemical-warfare laboratory. In his much-publicized book, Mirzayanov sets out the formulas for the claimed substances. According to the March 16 *Wall Street Journal*, that publicity led to the novichoks' chemical structure being leaked, making them readily available for reproduction elsewhere. Ralf Trapp, a France-

Boris Johnson, British Secretary of State for Foreign Affairs.

based consultant and expert on the control of chemical and biological weapons, told the *Journal*, "The chemical formula has been publicized and we know from publications from then-Czechoslovakia that they had worked on similar agents for defense in the 1980s. I'm sure other countries with developed programs would have as well."

But it does not seem that those "other countries" include Russia. The Organization for the Prohibition of Chemical Weapons (OPCW), the independent agency charged by treaty with investigating claims like those just made by the British government, certified in September 2017 that the Russian government had destroyed its entire chemical weapons program, inclusive of its nerve agent production capabilities. In addition to Trapp's account, Seamus Martin, writing in the March 14 *Irish Times*, posits, based on personal knowledge, that novichoks were widely expropriated by East Bloc oligarchs and criminal elements in the Russian economic chaos of the 1990s.

Thus, after being disclosed by a dissident Russian chemist living in the United States, novichoks have been widely copied by other countries, according to the press accounts.

Further trouble for May's attempted hoax is found in the condition of the Skripals and of a police officer who went to their home. All were made critically ill, although they are still alive. Yet the emergency personnel who treated the Skripals, allegedly the victims of a deadly and absolutely lethal nerve poison, suffered no ill effects whatsoever.

The Skripal poisoning is being compared in the British press to the poisoning of Alexander Litvinenko in 2006. The former KGB and FSB officer was granted asylum in London and worked for the infamous anti-Putin British-intelligence-directed oligarch Boris Berezovsky in information warfare and other attacks on the Russian state, inclusive of McCarthyite accusations against any European politician seeking sane relations with Putin.

Litvinenko's case officer was none other than Christopher Steele, and Christopher Steele conducted MI6's investigation of the case, which, of course, found Putin himself culpable. Berezovsky's use of the disgraced British PR firm Bell, Pottinger is also credited with a significant role in public acceptance of this result. Berezovsky was a prime suspect in organizing the murder of American journalist Paul Kleb-

British Labour Party leader Jeremy Corbyn.

nikov. Many believe that Berezovsky arranged Litvinenko's demise. Berezovsky himself died in Britain in mysterious circumstances following the loss of a major court case to another Russian oligarch, Roman Abramovich.

In the parliamentary debate in which Theresa May issued her provocation, opposition leader Jeremy Corbyn cautioned against a rush to judgment and pointed to the bloody playing field of Russian oligarchs and Russian organized crime as alternative areas for investigation. Had Corbyn added to that mix, "Western intelligence agencies," he would have been entirely on the right track. Corbyn also pointed out that these oligarchs had contributed millions to May's Conservative Party. The reaction by the British media, May's Conservatives, and Tony Blair's faction of the Labour Party was to paint Corbyn as a Putin dupe, including photoshopped images of the Labour leader in a Russian winter hat in front of the Kremlin.

The insane McCarthyite reactions to Corbyn's simple statements of fact show that he hit the nail on the head. If you want to find Skripal's poisoners, then, like Edgar Allen Poe, you must take in the whole picture first. The field of play involves the British intelligence services and the anti-Putin Russian oligarchs, each of which services the other, acting on behalf of British strategic objectives. It is no accident that the coup against Donald Trump and the latest British intelligence fraud, putting the entire world in peril, absolutely intersect one another.

China's Magnificent High-Speed Rail System

by Michael Billington

March 19—That China has the most advanced and most extensive high-speed rail system in the world is well known. The Chinese system originally gained support and technology from Germany's Siemens, France's Alstom, Canada's Bombardier, and Japan's Kawasaki, but is now producing its own train sets of the highest quality. What is less well known are the numerous ingenious systems China has developed *de novo* in order to become the world leader in rail technology, and by far the largest and fastest producer of high-speed rail in the world. This includes production technologies, testing technologies, construction techniques, machinery, and more.

Xinhua/Wei Wanzhong

A high-speed train in Guangxi Zhuang Autonomous Region of China.

It is difficult to overstate the amazing scope of the system. As of early 2018, China has constructed 22,000 km of domestic high-speed rail track, which is nearly double the total for the rest of the world combined. Not a single kilometer of rail in the United States would be counted as "high-speed" by China's standard—minimally 250 km/hr. (The Acela Express on the U.S. Northeast Corridor has a maximum speed, seldom attained, of just under 250 km/hr.) New high-speed rail is coming on line in China at the rate of 2,000 km/yr.

The fastest passenger train in the world, which also carries the most passengers per year, is the Beijing to Shanghai line. At 350 km/hr, it carries about 6 million passengers per year. The longest high-speed line in the world, to be completed in 2018, will run 2,230 km from Beijing to Guangzhou and Hong Kong.

The Beijing-Shanghai line was restricted to 300 km/hr after a major high-speed rail accident in 2011 in Wenzhou, Zhejiang Province, which killed 40 people and forced a re-evaluation and upgrading of the entire national system. In June 2017 the train sets running on the Beijing-Shanghai line were replaced by a higher standard system, fully designed and produced within China, called Fuxing (Rejuvenation), replacing the

Hexie (Harmony) trains which were commissioned in 2008. In early 2018, the speed limit for this line was raised back to 350 km/hr, and could eventually be raised to 400 km/hr, making the 1,318 km trip in just over three hours.

As recently as the 1990s, the average speed of China's trains was less than 60 km/hr.

A high-speed line from Lanzhou in Gansu Province to Urumqi in the far western Xinjiang Uygur Autonomous Region was opened in 2014, reducing the travel time from 21 hours to 8. Together with the New Silk Road Economic Belt, connecting China through Central Asia to Europe and Southwest Asia, this modern fast rail system has facilitated the development of the vast, under-populated far west regions of China, just as the opening of the first rail connection to Lhasa in 2006 facilitated the economic development of Tibet.

The line to Urumqi passes through multiple extremes of weather conditions, from broiling desert to snow-capped mountains—an 80 degree Centigrade

High-speed train in an urban setting in China.

temperature differential, which required the development of new materials and machinery. It also passes through the "hundred-*li* wind zone" in Shanshan, part of the Taklamakan Desert in Xinjiang, where desert winds blow almost every day of the year. They even knocked over a train in 2007. A 462 km wind-protection barrier was constructed next to the tracks of the high-speed line as it passes through the Gobi and Taklamakan desert regions.

The high-speed routes are only one-sixth of the total rail track in the country, but already they carry 60% of the passengers. The original plan, called 4+4 for four north-south routes and four east-west routes, is essentially complete as of the beginning of 2018. Now in the planning stages is an 8+8 system.

Financing the System

Only a few of the high-speed routes are currently profitable. Although over time that will change, it is not the top priority. Keeping prices reasonable to facilitate travel for all, to "serve the people," is far more important to the government. During the Spring Festival, the 40-day period in which millions of Chinese return to their home towns, 385 million people were travelling in China, many on the high-speed rail lines.

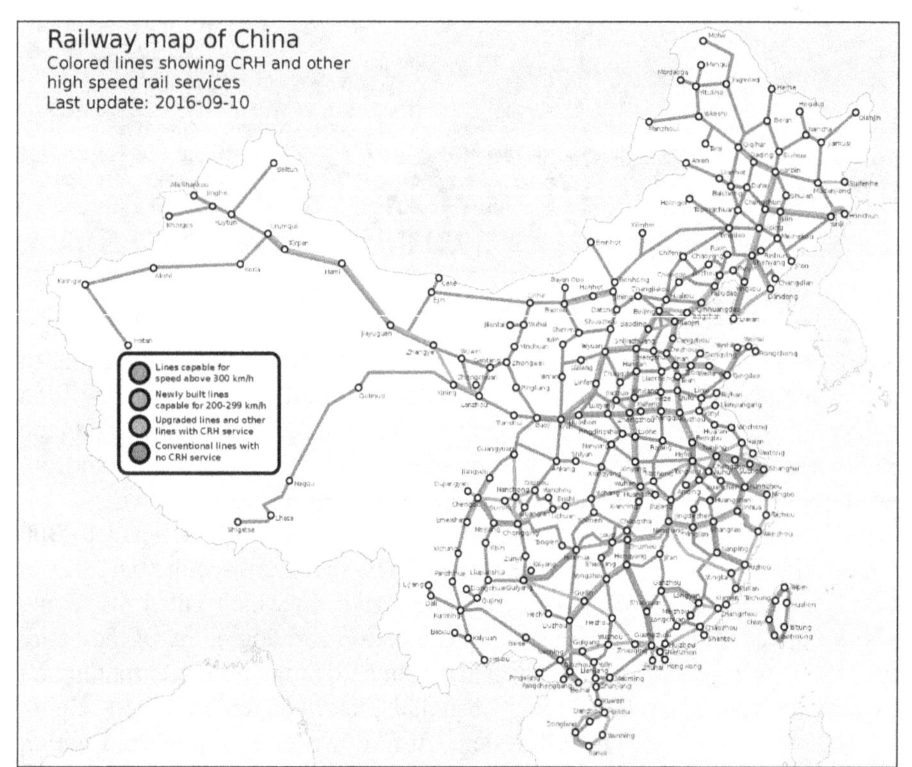

Machine in China enabling rapid placement of elevated trestles.

But it is also true that this system creates a dramatic boost in the productivity of the Chinese workforce due to enhanced mobility, which more than makes up for the lack of short-term profits for the fully government-owned system.

The famous magnetic levitation system which now connects Shanghai to its airport in Pudong using a German design—the only commercially active maglev in the world—has not been dramatically expanded for intercity travel as was once considered, but maglev is now being deployed for lower-speed intracity transit, using a system entirely developed within China.

Innovation in Every Aspect

A 50-minute documentary produced in October 2006 by China's CCTV on the high-speed rail system provides a fascinating look at the many levels of innovation that are the basis of China's world leadership in high-speed rail.

In order to pass over many rivers and canals, and through many cities, especially on the densely populated eastern coast rail routes, it rapidly became apparent that, in many cases, nearly the entire route would need to be constructed on viaducts rather than on the ground. An ingenious machine was designed to place each bridge span into place on the pillars for these viaducts, vastly reducing the time for construction. See it at work in the above link to the full video, or watch this five minute excerpt.

The Beijing-Shanghai line includes the longest bridge in the world, the Danyang-Kunshan Grand Bridge, passing over land and water. It is a 164.8 km viaduct constructed with the machine described above, including a 9 km section across Yangcheng Lake in the beautiful city of Suzhou in Jiangsu Province.

The required smoothness of the rails for high-speed rail is far greater than for regular trains, as the speed intensifies the impact of any imperfection. To make virtually seamless rail, 12 welding facilities were constructed across China, which bring in 100-meter-long rail sections (eight times longer than traditional rails), welding five of them together by robotic welders to near-perfect smoothness. The 500-meter rails are then lifted by 36 synchronized cranes onto special trains and delivered to the construction sites for the final welding.

Youtube

Danyang-Kunshan Grand Bridge in China.

High-speed train in China.

Testing facilities for various aspects of the high-speed trains also required innovation. In addition to wind tunnels to test for aerodynamics, a system for testing the wheel and rail quality was constructed using a 10-ton, three-meter diameter steel flywheel to test the wear on wheels and rail at 500 km/hr. The CCTV video describes the facility as the "most advanced testing equipment for high-speed trains in the world."

At another site, another large steel flywheel was constructed to test different qualities of metals to be used for the pantographs—the jointed framework above the train which conveys the electric current from overhead wires at speeds up to 500 km/hr.

And, described as the most secret of the innovations for the system, a "clean room" was constructed with a maximum of 10 mini-particles per cubic meter of air. In these rooms are produced the complex computer chips which run the trains and connect all the trains in the entire system to control centers.

The Belt and Road

China's world leadership in high-speed rail is not being kept for itself. As part of the Belt and Road Initiative, China is actively constructing or planning high-speed rail lines, as well as traditional rail lines, around the world. Laos, Thailand, Indonesia, Kenya, and Ethiopia already have systems in use or under construction. Trans-continental rail lines are in active planning stages in Africa and South America, as well as rail connections between the major cities in each of these two continents, ending the European colonial policy, which only built rail lines from the mines to the ports to extract raw materials, while leaving the countries themselves undeveloped and unconnected to each other.

The Chinese saying, "If you want to be rich, first build a road," characterizes their new paradigm approach: build the infrastructure as the necessary base for development. The proof is there for all to see in China.

High-speed trains in Wuhan prepared for the Spring Festival rush.

Italy Forty Years after Moro's Assassination— The Truth is Beginning to Come Out

by Claudio Celani

The following article appeared in EIR Strategic Alert, *number 12.*

March 16—Forty years ago, on March 16, 1978, the Italian statesman and Christian Democratic leader Aldo Moro was kidnapped by the terrorist Red Brigades, who killed the five policemen in his escort, and eventually killed Moro on May 9, after a 55-day captivity. Moro's assassination was a watershed in Italian politics, but the full truth revealing who was behind it, still has not come out into the open.

Aldo Moro was kidnapped as he was driving to Parliament, where a vote of confidence was expected for the "National Solidarity" government he had masterminded, which was led by Moro's party colleague Giulio Andreotti, and was for the first time based on a coalition including the Italian Communist Party (PCI).

Giulio Andreotti (left) with Aldo Moro.

wikipedia

A 2017 parliamentary investigative committee concluded that what we could call "an acceptable truth that was permissable to be uttered," had been established to cover up the Moro operation, by persons including Red Brigade members, and sections of the judiciary, police, and intelligence services. This "utterable truth" insists that no external agency steered or influenced the Red Brigades terrorists, who acted purely on the basis of their ideology alone.

Instead, the parliamentary committee concluded that the Red Brigades had been supported by several external agencies, and that the elimination of Moro must be seen in the strategic context of Italy's role in the Mediterranean and Middle East. Indeed, Andreotti's new Grand Coalition government had ensured strong parliamentary support for development policies in the Mediterranean, which crossed a red line for some European powers.

This strategic picture has emerged through the groundbreaking investigative work of journalist and author Giovanni Fasanella, who found documents in British archives proving that the British already considered Moro a "mortal enemy" by 1976, and had decided to stop him by any means necessary. Fasanella has published several books on the Moro case, including the most recent, *The Moro Puzzle*, which hit the bookstands just a few days before the March 16 anniversary.

The "unutterable truth," Fasanella writes in the introduction, "is that Moro's assassination was a real act of war against Italy, even though carried out by friendly and allied states—an attack against the sovereignty of the nation and its political freedom, led by foreign interests with the complicity of domestic fifth columns."

Documents Fasanella found in British archives show that Her Majesty's Government had discussed the option of a coup d'état to stop Aldo Moro in 1976, but rejected it in favor of "another option." According to Fasanella, one such "other option" was the Red Brigades terrorists.

This is also the opinion of former Socialist Party leader Claudio Signorile, who during Moro's 55 days

Aldo Moro being held by the terrorist Red Brigades.

of captivity, led negotiations with figures close to the Red Brigades for Moro's freedom.

In a recent interview, Signorile said that British influence on the Red Brigades started "in 1976, when [British] attention towards what was happening in Italy became much stronger. This is stated in the documents found in British archives, where they talk about a subversive action to be implemented to stop the ongoing process. One of the instruments might have been the Red Brigades."

It was the LaRouche movement that first pointed the finger at the British as being behind Moro's assassination. Only a few months after Moro's murder, in September 1978, LaRouche's Italian collaborators in the Partito Operaio Europeo (POE) published a special report entitled "Who Killed Aldo Moro" (*Chi Ha Ucciso Aldo Moro*), eloquently featuring a photomontage showing the British flag on the wall behind a photo of Aldo Moro as prisoner of the Red Brigades.

The political restoration after Moro's death, and especially after the 1992-93 destruction of the political system through "anti-corruption" investigations, has ensured that the "unutterable truth" remains buried. Today, all the Red Brigades terrorists are free, and some have even become successful authors. Matters have reached such grotesque dimensions that Barbara Balzerani, a member of the Red Brigades commando unit that kidnapped and killed Moro, was permitted to insult the victims in a public conference, after using Facebook to call for a party (in France) to celebrate the anniversary of March 16, 1978.

However, as the "unutterable truth" comes more and more into the open, the terrorists and their masters may soon stop laughing.

The scene of the Aldo Moro kidnapping, where his five bodyguards were killed.

'The British Empire Is Now Fully Exposed: It Must Be Crushed!'

This is the edited transcript of the Thursday, March 15, 2018 Schiller Institute New Paradigm webcast interview with the founder of the Schiller Institutes, Helga Zepp-LaRouche. She was interviewed by Harley Schlanger. A video of the webcast is available.

Harley Schlanger: Hello. I'm Harley Schlanger. Welcome to this week's Schiller Institute webcast, featuring our founder, Helga Zepp-LaRouche.

Extraordinary, fast-breaking developments are happening by the hour, confirming what we've been saying on this program over the last several weeks. The imperial geopoliticians will not let their system go without a big fight. Not surprisingly, we're seeing at the center of the fight forces in the United Kingdom coming into the open, who have taken the fight against Russia up a notch by blaming the Russians for the poisoning of a former Russian operative, Sergei Skripal. Helga what's the latest you have on this?

Helga Zepp-LaRouche: I think this is characterized quite correctly by the former British ambassador to Uzbekistan, Craig Murray. He said this is another attempt, like the fraudulent claims of Iraqi weapons of mass destruction—this time personally blaming Putin for being behind this assassination attempt against Skripal and his daughter.

Now, this story is not credible: Mr. Murray reports that according to Dr. Robin Black, formerly of the UK Porton Down research laboratory and a former member of the Organization for the Prohibition of Chemical Weapons (OPCW) Scientific Advisory Board, the actual existence of this alleged poison gas, Novichok, has never been proven. The OPCW has not included it on the list of banned substances, because the OPCW has never seen it; it has never been investigated. The

Russian Foreign Ministry spokesperson Maria Zakharova countered Prime Minister May's accusation.

OPCW does not have it. For the British government to immediately state that it has absolute proof that this has come from Russia, and it is definitely this substance, when it has nothing to compare it with, is really not a believable story. I think it really is, as the Russians said, an outrageous provocation. When an operation like this is run, the question is: what is the purpose of this?

Russian Foreign Minister Sergei Lavrov immediately said the charge against Russia has no substance. The spokeswoman of the Foreign Ministry, Maria Zakharova, immediately said this is an insane accusation; there is absolutely no proof. The British gave an ultimatum to Russia, giving Russia one day to explain how this substance came from Russia into Great Britain. The rules of the OPCW are that if any such case erupts, the accused country has ten days to respond. In that time samples have to be given to the accused party so that they can be investigated. All of this did not take place.

So, this is completely unusual behavior on the part

of the accusers, and I think it stinks to high heaven.

Schlanger: Part of the background is that the government of British Prime Minister May is in big trouble in Britain. Her government has not been exactly stable. But at the same time, British intelligence is now in the spotlight for the role it played through Christopher Steele, and the Steele dossier, in setting up Russiagate against President Trump. So this is not surprising that May is the one who's coming forward with this right now.

Zepp-LaRouche: Whenever you hear the name "Christopher Steele," you should remember that the U.S. House Intelligence Committee, after one year of investigation, found that there was no evidence of collusion of Trump with Russia. And remember, that accusation was entirely based on the Steele dossier.

So the fact that Christopher Steele has now emerged as a very prominent figure in this case of an alleged poison attack, is really quite stunning.

Mr. Skripal, a Russian agent who was "turned" in 1995, was turned by MI6 agent Pablo Miller. This whole operation of turning Skripal into a British double agent was apparently coordinated by Christopher Steele, who in that period was the head of MI6 Russia operations. Steele had also led the so-called investigation in the Litvinenko case, which has exactly the same profile as this present case. Steele left MI6 in 2009—now, "left" is in quotation marks, because it's a big question if he really left MI6, or if he was just outsourced into a so-called private security firm with the name of "Orbis Business Intelligence," whose main task ever since has been to produce so-called evidence of Russian operations—really accusations against Russia.

One of the operations run by Orbis was called Project Charlemagne, which claimed to have proof of Russian meddling into election campaigns in Great Britain, France, Germany, and Italy; of Russians financing Le Pen, Berlusconi, and the Alternative for Germany party

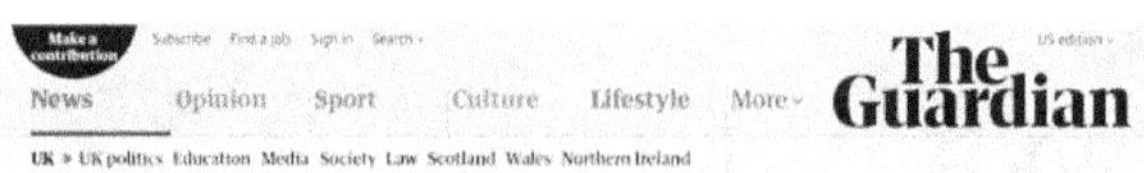

(AfD); and of alleged Russian operations to destroy the European Union. Orbis was also the place where the Steele dossier was produced. And, no surprise, Pablo Miller has also been working for Orbis.

Remember that many articles have appeared which demonstrate that Christopher Steele is not just some crazy guy who produced this filthy dossier about Trump. Former U.S. Foreign Service officer Peter van Buren had an article in the *American Conservative* which I would advise people to really re-read. He describes what a sophisticated intelligence operation Christopher Steele conducted, not only producing this dossier, for which Skripal may have been one of Steele's sources, but then creating so-called "secondary evidence" that was really his own leaks to the media, which were then used to corroborate reports to the FISA Court, as independent proofs of the original dossier. This article, "Christopher Steele: The Real Foreign Influence in the 2016 Election?" by Peter van Buren, very effectively reports how Steele's Russia dossier was part of a very sophisticated intelligence operation.

I find it stunning that Western governments—the German, French, and also the U.S. government—immediately backed up the British position with all of these questions still looming. I think this will not be the end of the story.

Mrs. May's actions remind me of the James Bond movies. Many people have probably seen at least one or two of these movies—remember that there is this character "M," who was James Bond's boss, who in several movies was played by Judy Dench. Mrs. May has certainly seen one too many of these movies. She probably thinks that she is "M," not in a James Bond movie but in real life, and is attempting to orchestrate a scenario, which eventually could lead to NATO Article 5 military action.

But, this is not a game; however I think it really is this kind of James Bond stuff. If you ever look at a James Bond movie again, ask yourself: what are they doing? They're terrorists! They're breaking the law, driving cars into crowds and shooting wildly. This is all the fantasy-driven realm of British intelligence. People should really take a second look at this, and start an investigation, asking: what is the British collusion in the Trump case and now, in the Skripal case?

Schlanger: Some people are asking why Trump—who himself is a target of British intelligence, who knows that the British have lied about him—would then sign on to a statement with Merkel and Macron that originated with British intelligence, which he knows is corrupt and immoral and a bunch of liars?

Another aspect of this is the media side of it, which takes us back to the Litvinenko case, which you mentioned. There's a British author, a reporter for *The Guardian*, Luke Harding, who wrote the so-called official book on the Litvinenko case, blaming it on Putin. He's written a book on Russia, called *The Mafia State*. And he also wrote a book recently called *Collusion: Secret Meetings, Dirty Money, and How Russia Helped Donald Trump Win*, which is a total defense of Christopher Steele.

So you see this is one network being deployed against the United States and against Russia. In the midst of this, at least in Britain, there was one fairly sound response which came from Labour Party leader Jeremy Corbyn. Do you have the remarks that he made, Helga?

Zepp-LaRouche: Yes, he made a speech in the House of Commons, where he warned against this, and demanded proof, saying that the relationship with Russia must be maintained.

Let me go to what you just said about Trump. *The Guardian* yesterday, before Trump signed on to this statement with Macron and Merkel, reported that Trump was reluctant to do that, because Trump knows perfectly well that it was British intelligence which was behind Russiagate for the last two years. So, I can only think that Trump is somewhat overwhelmed. He is surrounded by a lot of hyenas among the neo-cons and Wall Street, and that he does not yet have the kind of team together to really do what he wants to do. We are seeing a new facet of the effort to box Trump in, to get him into the anti-Russia camp, and I think it's a very dangerous situation.

I find it absolutely scandalous that Merkel and

UN/Loey Philipe

UK Deputy Permanent Representative to the UN, Jonathan Guy Allen (left) speaking with U.S. Permanent Representative to the UN, Nikki Haley, March 14, 2018.

Macron, who are not under such attack, immediately sided with the British. That should give German and French voters and citizens, real food for thought: Are these people helping to prepare what can only be described as a pre-war scenario?

Schlanger: Another example of this pre-war scenario is what's happening with Syria. U.S. UN Ambassador Nikki Haley and Former Secretary of State Rex Tillerson have come out saying that the Russians are to blame for the alleged use of chemical weapons in Syria, even though, just as in this Skripal case, there's no evidence that Assad was using chemical weapons.

So, Helga, I assume you see this whole operation in Syria coming to a head as part of this same anti-Russian commitment?

Zepp-LaRouche: When you bring up Nikki Haley—I keep thinking there is a certain type of American woman: Condoleezza Rice, Susan Rice, Samantha Power, and now Nikki Haley—are all from the same type of Gestalt. And it's really unfortunate that America would be represented by such women, especially in the United Nations.

Nikki Haley threatened an American attack on Damascus, which is pretty wild, and the Russian Chief of General Staff, Gen. Valery Gerasimov, immediately said that if the life of even one Russian soldier were threatened, Russia would take determined and adequate countermeasures. So, we are on the verge of an escalation in Syria.

This all has to do with the fact that the New Paradigm is winning, the old paradigm is shattered. A new strategic reality is emerging from the ever-expanding New Silk Road, which is progressively moving, now including more than 140 countries as Chinese Foreign Minister Wang Yi recently said in a press conference in Beijing.

Don't underestimate the impact of the March 1 speech by President Putin as part of this new strategic reality. Putin announced new weapons systems, the Mach 20 rocket, which does not depend on a ballistic trajectory but is highly maneuverable, and therefore can outmaneuver the ABM systems of the United

U.S. Department of State

Former U.S. Secretary of State Rex Tillerson, in Nigeria, March 12, 2018.

States; and also render impotent the stationing of U.S. troops close to Russia. This has created a new strategic reality: I think this British operation and the escalation in Syria are really rearguard battles of a system which is clearly failing.

Schlanger: Now, in the midst of this, Trump has fired Tillerson, bringing in CIA director Pompeo. Do you have any reading on that?

Zepp-LaRouche: I don't have an evaluation of Pompeo. I read an article that said his career was sponsored by the Koch brothers. We will have to see how this works out, if he will work with Trump. The problem was that Tillerson obviously didn't. The tension between President Trump and Tillerson had grown recently, over issues including North Korea and the approach to Syria. How long should U.S. troops stay in Syria? Trump had said U.S. troops have only one task, that is, to defeat ISIS and then return home. Tillerson said, no, we will stay there for a long time. Then Tillerson immediately, without any hesitation, backed May in her accusations against Russia. I think one of the really revealing signs that Tillerson had moved closer to the neo-cons in the recent period was that he, on his recent Africa trip, told every African country he visited to be watchful with respect to China; be careful, do not work with China. In Africa, that was, as you could expect, not exactly welcome. The Africans have seen very clearly who are their friends—who is investing, and who is improving their living conditions, and who is not.

All of this accumulated. Trump laid Tillerson off, and I think there is no reason to be unhappy about that.

Schlanger: Then we have the recent interesting comments from Defense Secretary Mattis in Afghanistan. One of the things Trump had promised, as a candidate, is that he would end the war in Afghanistan, and that the United States would not engage in these practices. It now appears that Mattis is putting forward what you might call the original Trump doctrine.

Zepp-LaRouche: I think this is a clear shift away from the last 16 years' policy of the U.S.A. with respect to Afghanistan, which has not led to any stabilization of that country. The idea that you have to have some kind of reconciliation between the government and the Taliban is one step in the right direction. The economic reconstruction of Afghanistan will then be immediately and urgently needed. President Ghani has requested help from China, Russia, India, and other countries. Extending the New Silk Road into Afghanistan will be the only way to get this done.

The Russians and the Iranians have, for a very long time, called for the reconciliation of the government and the Taliban. I think that that *is* one of the spots where something seems to be going in the right direction.

Schlanger: The other spot where things seem to be moving along is, more surprisingly, North Korea. It's clear that there's a very concerted effort, from Russia, China, and the United States, and possibly Japan and South Korea as well, toward a solution there. This, again, goes *against* what many people think, because most commentators were saying that Trump was about to start a war there. This is moving pretty quickly, don't you think?

Zepp-LaRouche: I think you can now really see who are the warmongers, and who are the people willing to work to resolve these conflicts through diplomacy and negotiations. The Democrats and most of the mainstream media have had insane responses, attacking it, saying this can never work, that it's a big mistake by Trump. But a few leading Democrats, such as Bill Richardson and former President Jimmy Carter, said this is absolutely the right thing to do; it's a good thing to try to solve this conflict through negotiations. And I think that today people are revealing themselves in a very stark manner.

Schlanger: Sixty-eight former members of the Obama Administration have formed something called National Security Action—ironically, NSA—which includes Susan Rice, Samantha Power, a lot of the old Clinton/Obama networks. They signed a statement which is essentially a war against Trump, complaining that Trump is not committed to war against Russia and China! How does the world look at something like this?

Zepp-LaRouche: This document is another piece of very useful reading material for anyone in the United States who is still nostalgic about President Obama, but also in Europe. This National Security Action group is blatantly mistaken. Obviously, that statement was written and published just before the breakthrough occurred with respect to the Korean Peninsula: they are completely off on that point. But their open call for confrontation with Russia and China is really an important lesson for anyone concerned about world peace: Who is the war party? It is definitely these Democrats from the Obama/Hillary Clinton period. And people who have nostalgia for Obama should really reflect on that. Do they want World War III? This statement is really bad. I think people should really rethink things. The Trump policy is, in part, very problematic. He has had a very difficult time, being under constant attack by these putschists all the time. So, I strongly urge people to reflect seriously on what I've just raised here.

Schlanger: Before we close, I want to give you a chance to say something about what seems to be the next phase of the soap opera here in Berlin, where the Merkel government has just been finalized. She's now got a fourth term, and yet, her government is still looking for something that its actually going to do.

German Chancellor Angela Merkel speaking to the German Bundestag.

Bundeskanzlerin.de

Zepp-LaRouche: I have never seen such despondent articles greeting a newly formed government. Even conservative papers like *Die Welt* referred to this situation as "Italian conditions." People are completely frustrated with this political class. It is constantly changing its political outlook. So, it's really a terrible beginning. Merkel only got 364 votes of the 399 votes held by members of the so-called "Grand Coalition," which is not so grand any more. They barely have a majority. The three parties comprising the coalition lost very significantly in the September general elections.

But the biggest problem is that they have no positive conceptions! They have no vision for the future; they want to stick to all the old rotten policies. The new finance minister, Olaf Scholz, is committed to staying with the "Black Zero" policy [of avoiding new public debt] of his predecessor Schäuble. Jens Spahn, the health minister, is from the pharmaceutical industry and has already made outrageous statements about the poor in Germany, provoking a wave of attacks. But that all reflects that they have absolutely no conception, which is really bad for Germany. I think the German people deserve a better government than that, but they have not learned that lesson quickly enough yet.

This makes the task for our organization all the clearer. We have to intervene with a clear vision: Germany should join the New Silk Road. We should do something against the pending danger of a new financial crash. We should implement Glass-Steagall. This means going back to the economic policies of the Kreditanstalt für Wiederaufbau in the postwar period, which was based on the Reconstruction Finance Corporation of Franklin D. Roosevelt. We, in Germany, do have a tradition of having a decent credit policy, but nothing like that is coming from this government. We, our work and our policies, are extremely necessary not only in Germany; but also in other European countries, because the Damocles sword of a new financial crash is hanging over the world.

We just talked to some insiders who said that beyond the $570 trillion in over-the-counter derivatives officially acknowledged by the bank for International Settlements, there is another $70 trillion in admitted derivatives contracts, which is obviously a powder keg which could blow up the monetary system at any moment.

I appeal to you, our viewers, to get in contact with us, become active, help us spread the idea of Glass-Steagall and the organization of the Four Laws which were proposed by my husband, Lyndon LaRouche, several years ago. We need increased discussion of the necessity of our nations joining the New Paradigm and absolutely abandoning this destructive geopolitical approach. I said it at the beginning of this year, *we must overcome geopolitics*, because in this era of thermonuclear weapons, no conflict should be solved, or can be solved, through military means. If you don't consider that, we are on the edge of World War III. What is coming from the British, right now, is useful only in one respect: It makes the role the British are playing absolutely clear. It has been going on the whole time, but now it is more out in the open than ever before. So, we should really move to end the British empire and replace it with a New Paradigm, a new set of international relations among nations based on sovereignty, on respect for other nations' social systems, and for the common aims of mankind. I think that debate is urgently needed.

Schlanger: And, as we've been pointing out throughout this discussion, the British are now fully exposed.

Helga, I want to end with an important question for you. I think you basically answered this just now, in a certain way, but I think it's worth revisiting, because this is such an overwhelming situation—there's so much happening, so much to be on top of, and the media, of course, are trying to demoralize people, to convince them there's nothing that can be done. What advice would you give to someone who wants to participate in the debate you're calling for? How should they be thinking about themselves and this moment in history?

Zepp-LaRouche: There are many subjects we could discuss, and many things we should do. The image people have about the West is really something people should think about. Why is it that China, which is a socialist country, based on "socialism with Chinese characteristics," as they put it—why is this country doing so much better than the West? That should be food for thought. What is wrong with the neo-liberal method, the system which is causing the gap between rich and poor to become wider all the time? I think in every European country—and the Trump election reflects that as well— many people are completely disgusted with the political class, with the class of the managers, bankers, and academia. People do not feel represented by these institutions any longer, which can be very dangerous. In Europe, it has given rise to some really very dangerous or at least problematic parties and organizations.

So the lack of reason is giving birth to monsters, as Goya pointed out so clearly in his drawings.

I think people should start to become active. You cannot sit by in a paradigm change like the one we are experiencing at this point. Become active; contact us, the Schiller Institute. Invite some of your friends and neighbors to discuss the subject we are raising here. You can speak with members of the Schiller Institute to discuss this further, to set up speaking engagements. You should start studying all of these issues in depth— don't just go by whatever the daily newspapers are trying to feed you. Try to develop your own thinking, to understand what Russia is really doing. Is Putin the demon the Western media are making him, or is Russian policy something totally different? Is Russian history totally different than you think? Is China maybe completely different?

Just don't fall for the kinds of prejudices which are being pre-cooked for you by the mainstream media every day. I think it's really time for everyone to take seriously becoming an independent thinker, having independent knowledge, and being able to form your own judgment; to search for the truth and become politically active. I think that that is the only advice I can give you.

Schlanger: I think that's pretty good advice and I hope people take it to heart.

Helga, thank you for joining us this week, and we'll be back again next week.

Zepp-LaRouche: Yes. Bye-bye.

hz.zepp@schiller-institut.de

Ms. 'M' Pulls Her Western Allies into a Dangerous Confrontation with Russia

by Helga Zepp-LaRouche, Chair of the German political party
Civil Rights Movement Solidarity (*Büso*)

March 17—It only took a single day, once Chancellor Angela Merkel had sworn, in her oath of office, "to protect the German people from harm," for her fully to support the irresponsible provocation of the British government against Russia, through the joint declaration of the governments of France, the United States, Great Britain, and Germany. Macron, Trump, May, and Merkel agreed that there was "no other plausible explanation" for the neurotoxin attack on former double agent Sergei Skripal and his daughter Julia, other than blaming Russia for it. This operation is so blatant that there is only one plausible explanation: The British Empire wants to involve the entire West in an escalation of the new Cold War and possibly more. And Mrs. Merkel jumps in without hesitation.

Meanwhile, a number of well-known experts have pointed out that the one-day ultimatum May gave to the Russian government, to clarify how the neurotoxin "Novichok" came from Russia to the United Kingdom, is a clear breach of the rules of the Organization for the Prohibition of Chemical Weapons (OPCW), of which the United Kingdom is also a member. It would have been necessary to give the OPCW samples of the substance for an independent analysis, after which the accused country, Russia, would have had ten days to comment on the allegation.

The former British ambassador to Uzbekistan, Craig Murray, characterized the "Novichok" story, for which the British government did not provide the slightest evidence, as a hoax in the tradition of the alleged "weapons of mass destruction of Iraq," which, as one may recall, was based on a memo from the British secret service, MI6. Murray also pointed out that Robin Black, the head of the only British factory that produces chemical weapons, emphasized in a prestigious scientific journal in 2016 that the evidence that this poison even exists is thin, and that its chemical composition was unknown. So, although Britain obviously did not have samples—and thus had nothing to compare to the poison used in the attack on Skripal—May claimed that only Russia could be responsible.

Incidentally, the British chemical weapons facility is located in Porton Down, interestingly enough just twelve kilometers from Salisbury, where the attack took place.

Xinhua /Han Yan
British Prime Minister Theresa May.

The Novichok Story Is Indeed Another Iraqi WMD Scam

As recently as 2016 Dr Robin Black, Head of the Detection Laboratory at the UK's only chemical weapons facility at Porton Down, a former colleague of Dr David Kelly, published in an extremely prestigious scientific journal that the evidence for the existence of Novichoks was scant and their composition unknown.

> In recent years, there has been much speculation that a fourth generation of nerve agents, 'Novichoks' (newcomer), was developed in Russia, beginning in the 1970s as part of the 'Foliant' programme, with the aim of finding agents that would compromise defensive countermeasures. Information on these compounds has been sparse in the public domain, mostly originating from a dissident Russian military chemist, Vil Mirzayanov. No independent confirmation of the structures or the properties of such compounds has been published. (Black, 2016)

Report by former British Ambassador to Uzbekistan, Craig Murray.

Because of its nebulous nature, the OPCW had not included Novichok in its list of chemical weapons.

Steele, Not Moscow

The story is even more interesting if one considers the role of Christopher Steele in the affair. Sergei Skripal, who was working for Russian military intelligence at the time, was apparently "turned" in 1995 by an MI6 agent named Pablo Miller, in an operation coordinated by Steele, who was then working under diplomatic cover in Moscow. When Steele "left" MI6 in 2009, he founded the private security firm "Orbis Business International," whose business plan is public-relations marketing of allegations against Russia. These have included "Project Charlemagne" on Russia's alleged interference in elections in France, Italy, Britain, and Germany; the alleged Russian funding of Le Pen, Berlusconi, and the Alternative for Germany (AfD); and an alleged Russian campaign to destroy the EU.

The absolute masterpiece of Steele's career as a spook, however, is the attempted coup against President Trump through the collusion between the Obama Administration intelligence chiefs, the Democratic Party (DNC) leadership, the Hillary Clinton campaign, and the British intelligence service, all based on the "dirty dossier" on Trump that Steele and Orbis had produced. The U.S. House Intelligence Committee has just announced the outcome of its more than year-long investigation: that there was absolutely no collusion between the Russian government and Trump.

Instead, Senators Grassley and Graham, in a letter to Attorney General Sessions and his deputy Rosenstein, have called for a Special Counsel to investigate the FBI and senior members of the Department of Justice on well-founded suspicion of collusion with British intelligence and with Steele in his special role. Thus the entire apparatus of the so-called "Deep State," the intelligence services' "state within the state" and its involvement with British intelligence, is in the crosshairs of the investigation by the U.S. Congress.

Peter van Buren, a 24-year high-ranking veteran of the U.S. State Department, emphasized the particular character of Steele's intervention in a Feb. 15 article in *The American Conservative*, entitled "Christopher Steele: The Real Foreign Influence in the 2016 Election?" Steele and his company Orbis not only produced the dossier allegedly proving that Trump owed his election victory to Putin, but he and various Orbis employees carried out an extremely professional operation to place this disinformation in the top institutions of the state and to launch a full information war against the American public. Steele had managed to create entire networks, which then provided so-called "independent" confirmations of his disinformation, which were then used to get surveillance of Trump

and his team approved by the responsible secret court.

Who else belonged to the Orbis team of this operation, who passed Steele's dossier to Trump's opponent John McCain during a conference in Canada? Sir Andrew Wood, the British Ambassador to Moscow during the same period that Miller's Skripal was "turned" under Steele's supervision. It should also be mentioned that Steele was later instructed by MI6 to be the official in charge of the allegations against Russia in the case of Alexander Litvinenko, the precursor of the Skripal case.

In other words, the same circle of "former" MI6 operatives responsible for the propaganda operation on Trump's alleged collusion with Russia, which is now discredited as fake news, is at the center of the Skripal attack. If it waddles like a duck, quacks like a duck, and looks like a duck, it's most likely a duck—that is, a British intelligence operation.

Propaganda Campaign Towards World War

Russian Foreign Minister Lavrov commented on the anti-Russian hysteria of the West at a Moscow forum entitled "Russia, a Land of Opportunities," with these words: "What we are experiencing right now is that the United States and its western allies are aware that the 500-year period of Western dominance of world politics is coming to an end." The transition to a new multipolar, democratic, and just world order will take a long time, but it is already painful for those who have been accustomed for centuries to ruling the world.

Exactly the same arrogance of power was the reason that for four years the neo-liberal establishment underestimated the enormous dynamic of the New Silk Road initiative of China, which now has 140 participating nations—only to react all the more hysterically to the fact that now this new paradigm dominates the world. For the same reason, this establishment underestimated Russia's re-emergence under Putin, who demonstrated in his March 1 speech, with the presentation of new weapons systems based on new physical principles, that Russia is not merely a "regional power," but has in fact surpassed the West in some technological areas.

Instead of reacting to these new strategic realities with methods from the dirty bag of tricks of the secret services, or endorsing these methods with "solidarity statements," we need a redefinition of our own politics. Instead of viewing the New Silk Road as a threat to a

Prime Minister Theresa May at a joint press conference with German Chancellor Angela Merkel in Berlin, February 16, 2018.

unipolar world which is no longer possible, we should accept China's offer of win-win cooperation. The ongoing, absolutely hysterical campaigns against Russia and China are obvious prewar propaganda for a new world war in which the loser can only be all of humanity.

Instead of being downgraded to the status of a colony of the British Empire, Germany should make a decisive contribution to shaping the future of one humanity's common destiny, of which President Xi Jinping always speaks. We could contribute our great tradition of German classical culture and the heritage of all our poets, thinkers and inventors, to shaping a more human future.

If we take up the offer of cooperation with the New Silk Road, as the Eastern, Central, and Southern European states, and the Balkan countries, Switzerland, and Austria have already done, we can not only rebuild the Middle East economically, together with Russia and China, and develop the African continent—solving the refugee crisis in the only possible humane way—but we can also build a new global security architecture based on economic integration. However, if the established political class in this country is unable to reflect on a perspective that can guarantee the long-term survival of our nation, then all thinking people should urgently work to ensure that cooperation with the New Silk Road is on the agenda.

If Ms. Theresa May feels she must imitate Judi Dench as "M" in a James Bond movie, that only betrays her bad taste. To be drawn into a confrontation with Russia by such a model is irresponsible.

zepp-larouche@eir.de

A Philosophy for Victory: Can We Change the Universe?

by Lyndon H. LaRouche, Jr.[1]

Foreword

At a Washington, D.C. meeting in mid-February 1983, I warned the Soviet government, and also relevant high levels of our own, that unless President Reagan were to offer what the President later did announce as a Strategic Defense Initiative (SDI), and unless the Soviet government were to accept such an offer, the Soviet economic system was doomed to collapse in about five years. I repeated that forecast many times, publicly, during the course of the 1980s. The President made that offer,[2] and the Soviet government rejected it peremptorily. The consequent collapse of the Soviet economic system took about six years, not five.

In a Berlin press conference of October 12, 1988, which was nationally-televised in the U.S. shortly after that, I forecast the imminence of a chain-reaction collapse of the Soviet economic system, an already onrushing collapse, which would lead toward the probable reunification of Germany in the short-term period immediately ahead.[3] I proposed a policy for dealing with that crisis.

My policy of October 1988 was later elaborated as the "European Productive Triangle" program of 1990,[4] and expanded and promulgated as the "Eurasian Landbridge" program crafted by my associates during 1992-1993.[5]

Unfortunately, by the combined decision of Britain's Prime Minister Margaret Thatcher, France's President François Mitterrand, and President George Bush, a policy was adopted, which was directly opposite to what I had proposed at Berlin in October 1988. As a result of the 1989-2001 continuation of those policies, aimed at ruining the economies of both Germany and the former Comecon states, which were jointly launched by Thatcher, Mitterrand, and Bush during 1989-90, not only has the former Soviet power collapsed, but the world's economy as a whole is presently at the brink of the most disastrous economic collapse in modern history.[6]

In my warnings, during the 1982-1983 period leading up to President Ronald Reagan's March 23, 1983 announcement, I had emphasized that the military side of my proposal for strategic ballistic-missile defense, was only the surface of the strategic policy I was proposing. Both the U.S. and Soviet economies were then already far advanced in their decay, down from the levels of long-term physical vitality both had commanded until about the mid-1960s.[7] Without a "crash"

---

1. The author is a registered candidate for the 2004 U.S. Presidential nomination.

2. National TV network broadcast, March 23, 1983.

3. This forecast proved entirely correct.

4. Jonathan Tennenbaum et al., ***Das 'Produktive Dreieck' Paris-Berlin-Wien: Ein europäisches Wirtschaftswunder als Motor für die Weltwirtschaft*** (Wiesbaden: EIR Nachrichtenagentur GmbH, August 1990); "The Economic Geography of Europe's 'Productive Triangle,'"

Originally published in EIR, *March 2, 2001.*

EIR, August 3, 1990;

5. Organizing around this report began about 1993. A full report was issued June 9, 1991, as an *EIR* Special Report, "Can Europe Stop the World Depression?"

6. LaRouche's "Ninth Forecast" was published in *EIR*, June 24, 1994, under the title "The Coming Disintegration of Financial Markets." For the policy implications of the confirmation of that forecast by subsequent events, see also Lyndon H. LaRouche, Jr., "Trade Without Currency," *EIR*, August 4, 2000.

7. A useful date of reference, would be British Prime Minister Harold

www.arttoday.com

EIRNS/Stuart Lewis

kind of science-driver program, akin to the economically successful Kennedy space-program, both the U.S. and Soviet economy were self-doomed to that collapse inhering in their respective, current policies of economic practice. The most notable difference in their situation, was that the risk of a Soviet collapse, was relatively more immediate at that tim e, than the prospect for an ensuing U.S. economic collapse. The only feasible medium- to long-term alternatives for such collapses, was a "crash program" type of science-driver upturn, which would be intended, and gauged to reverse the damage already done to the world's physical economy by the policy-changes of the 1966-1983 interval.

Thus, I had argued, since even two years earlier than my strategic-defense proposal of Summer 1979, that the need of both super-powers for economic recovery vastly outweighed the adversarial issues between them. Yes, we should free the world from the grip of strategic-missile blackmail, but we should use the need for such a defense as the pivot for a global

---

Wilson's pound sterling collapse of Fall 1967, and the ensuing March crisis of the U.S. dollar.

"crash economic-recovery" effort, from which both sides would benefit.

The essential difference between the 1989-1991 collapse of the Soviet system, and the presently onrushing collapse of the world economy of the Anglo-American powers, was chiefly in their timing. Both have been on the road to collapse since about the time of President Richard Nixon's 1966-68 election-campaign.

Looking back to my Washington, D.C. discussions of February 1983, the correct view of the world situation today, is expressed by saying that "Two economic systems have collapsed. Russia is now struggling to rebuild itself out of the wreckage left by the collapsed and carpet-bagger-looted Soviet system; the Anglo-American system is now at its fag-end." Still, after all that, the ruling monetary powers of today's world are, chiefly, engaged in desperately defending a post-1971 world monetary system which was always foredoomed to fail, and has now reached the advanced stage of the crisis, under President George W. Bush, that that world system could not be saved in its present form. even for a relatively short-term period.

So, today, we are assembled here, under the auspices of the written word, to consider, *not* whether the continued existence of the United States is still possible; the question is, whether it is possible that the United States might choose the available road to survival. Classical philosophy, properly defined, is the only branch of science in which possible solutions to such a crisis in decision-making can be rationally discussed.

The leading founders of the United States, and their forerunners, such as Benjamin Franklin and Cotton Mather, would have agreed with my emphasis upon philosophy. Sometimes, to survive, one must know how to swim. The problem today, is the relatively vast numbers from recent crops of university trained professionals, in or outside high positions in government, who, like the "Ozymandias" from Shelley's poem, neither know how to swim in the waters of Classical philosophy, nor would be willing to learn, even if the survival of their nation depended upon it.

As in many other matters, today's universities, and their textbooks, have degraded what is taught under the rubric of "philosophy," into the categories of teachings which are, usually, disgustingly trivial when they are not actually evil. Thus, as Shakespeare's Doll Tearsheet spoke of Ancient Pistol's title of "Captain," so she might have spoken of the name of philosophy today: "God's light, these villains will make the word as odious as the word occupy; which was an excellent good word until it was ill-sorted."[8] It were often necessary, as today, in dealing with serious matters at hand, to substitute another term for the misused name of philosophy: *epistemology*, the matter of the often hidden axioms of assumption which underlie the entirety of specific systems of thought. In the alternative, we might do as I do here, to use other ways to make the relevant distinctions sufficiently clear, that we have no need to seek a substitute for the name of philosophy.

So, if we are to understand the real universe in which cultures, even great empires, destroy themselves, we must begin, as I do here, by making a sharp, uncompromising distinction between my own choice, of historically rooted, Classical use of those terms, and that contrary, trivial or worse, use which is commonplace among the intellectual "bottom feeders," the existentialists, pragmatists, empiricists, and logical positivists, of today's academic life.

Despite all else, the term "philosophy" ought to be recognized as signifying the most important conception to be mastered, in attempting to deal with the menacing reality of current world history, even in the short term. The possibility of a continued existence of civilization, even in the relatively near term, depends absolutely upon leaders who govern themselves with obligatory attention to the practical significance of thinking philosophically, as I define philosophy here.

Thus, the following pages address a subject-matter which must be resolved as a philosophical problem of great urgency, a subject which must be addressed, as I do here, for the sake of the possible survival of the recently existing global civilization. For purpose of this review, I emphasize the form which the crisis assumes for the specific type of *globally extended modern European civilization*, focussing chiefly upon the immediate, short-term interval of the escalating global crisis currently in progress.[9]

The most important, and most fundamental of the issues posed to us by this onrushing catastrophe, is: *As a matter of principle, to what degree, in what manner, and by what means, can man gain foreknowledge of the method by which to willfully change the current direction of his society's destiny, for the better, in specific ways? Even to overcome, thus, the worst sort of impending, seemingly inevitable catastrophe, such as the presently onrushing one?*

Threatened by the present, overwhelming likelihood of a collapse of civilization, into a planetary new dark age of humanity, how might *we* change what I shall define here as the presently characteristic behavior of mankind, to bring this civilization to safety, even within the relatively short term?

I write here as a spokesman for what is sometimes called "the American intellectual tradition," that Euro-

---

8. I.e., "fell into bad company." William Shakespeare, ***King Henry IV: Second Part***, Act II, Scene IV.

9. The distinguishing characteristic of European civilization, is the combination of the Classical Greek cultural legacy, especially that of Plato, and Christianity. This is extended through the spread of Islam, which shares with Christianity, and the Mosaic tradition of Philo of Alexandria and of Moses Mendelssohn, the conception of man and woman as made equally in the image of the Creator of the universe, and as specifically empowered to rule over all things within that universe. Other cultures, especially among those in Asia, do not necessarily proceed from that image of the nature of man specific to the European expression of the Judeo-Christian-Islamic current deeply embedded in globally extended modern European civilization. However, since European civilization is the world's most powerful culture, as measurable in per capita terms, the fate of the world as a whole is set in the context of the crisis within globally extended modern European civilization.

pean Classical tradition expressed in the writing of our 1776 Declaration of Independence and the Preamble of our Federal Constitution. Those institutions I defend, and see any proposal to consider superseding them, as far worse than useless, at present, or during the foreseeable future. The cause for our nation's current self-afflictions lies in influences which have been contrary to that American intellectual tradition.[10]

The root of our current crisis, lies in the way in which policies contrary to that American intellectual tradition, have been brought to hegemonic positions, where they have lately ruled and ruined our national policy-shaping institutions. It is those superimpositions, alien to that tradition, which are ruining us. Therefore, no action possible within a framework limited to the currently hegemonic, errant policy-making assumptions of our government and most other influential institutions, could have any net effect but to ensure, even worsen the presently onrushing catastrophe.

I denounce not only the present policies of our government, or political parties, for example. Under lately corrupting, even implicitly treasonous trends, especially those of the recent thirty-five-odd years rise of Nixon's "Southern Strategy," our nation's policy-shaping errors have become *systemic*. Our nation's presently threatened doom, is neither accidental nor cyclical; it is systemic, as merely typified by increasingly demented qualities of public utterances by the presently panic-stricken Federal Reserve Chairman Alan Greenspan.[11]

By *systemic crisis*, I mean that we must uproot and replace many among the implied set of axioms which currently govern the selection of the kinds of changes in policy which those institutions, and prevailing public opinion, would be presently willing to tolerate. The possibility of surviving this crisis, depends upon selecting the right answers to the question: *Which adopted or* *implied axioms of present policy-shaping behavior of our government, and citizenry, must we replace, and replace with what, to bring about the needed, early change in direction toward survival and recovery of both the U.S.A. and civilization generally?*

---

1. The Issue of Historical Method

Given the fact, that man is a creature distinguished from the beasts by his free will, nothing is "in the cards." In a truly sane society, there is no place of influence over policy-making, given to crystal-ball gazers, contemporary astrologers, "Biblical prophecy" windbags, or the like. So, the doctrine of "historical objectivity" preached by socialists such as the early Twentieth Century's Kautsky and Plekhanov, for example, in claiming a certain kind of fatal, so-called "objective," so-called "anti-voluntarist" ordering of history, never produced anything but ultimately catastrophic results for their followers, during that time. A similar outcome awaited such later followers of the same, virtually mechanistic doctrine of "historical objectivity," as Soviet leaders Brezhnev, Andropov, and Gorbachev.

Once we acknowledge, that man is distinguished, *systemically*, from both the non-living and the beasts, by free will, there are, nonetheless, bounds which define what nature will, or will not tolerate from man's free will. Free will is not the right of individuals, or even majorities of entire societies, to make arbitrary choices. As I shall present the case in the following pages, free will is a higher principle of law, otherwise called *reason*, or *natural law*.

There are special, higher qualities of universal lawfulness, operating at a higher level than the non-living aspects of our universe, or even higher than living processes other than the human species. These higher qualities of universal lawfulness, govern the way in which man is variously allowed, or punished for attempting to change the universe in which our species exists. It is that higher lawfulness, which we must adduce, if we are to become capable of foreseeing the most important of the consequences which our decisions, or lack of changes in habits, might bring about. Therefore, my use of "free will" is a qualified one; in my hands, it means that form of "free will" which coheres with that higher lawfulness which I have defined repeatedly, in published locations, as *a universal principle of physical-economic anti-entropy*.

---

10. A notable example is former Secretary of State Henry A. Kissinger, who described himself explicitly as a proud foe of that "American intellectual tradition," in a London Chatham House keynote address of May 10, 1982, "Reflections on a Partnership: British and American Attitudes to Postwar Foreign Policy, Address in Commemoration of the Bicentenary of the Office of Foreign Secretary," as he had represented himself similarly in his *A World Restored: Metternich, Castlereagh and the Problems of Peace 1812-1822* (Boston: Houghton-Mifflin, 1957). He stressed that this had been his position while Secretary of State and National Security Advisor to Presidents Richard Nixon and Gerald Ford.

11. The most appropriate documentation of Greenspan's tendency to disintegrate before TV cameras, appeared after the foregoing lines were written, in his appearance before the Congress on Tuesday, Feb. 13, 2001. In the popular vernacular of today, "This man has really lost it!"

Such were the issues of the Classical controversy between the heroic Prometheus, and tragic figure of the doomed, satanic oligarch Zeus and his gods of Olympus, in Aeschylus' *Prometheus Bound*. That is the underlying nature of the crisis, which threatens to bring about the early doom of our United States under President George W. Bush, today. That latter, is the determining, underlying issue referenced by the subject of this report.

How shall we, then, select only those aspects of implicitly revolutionary, "free will" changes in the axioms governing policy-making, which represent a positive factor in the shaping of history?

Thus, the direction being taken by a society, is often flanked by the swamps defined by such lunatic extremes as either arbitrary, existentialist kinds of choices, or capitulation to fatalism. There are discoverable pathways, leading upward from such perilous terrain, as that into which careless opinion has presently misled most nations. The point is, to know how to instruct free will in selecting society's appropriate, *axiomatic* choices of historic pathway.

This view and practice of the making of history, is what I have defined as a scientific basis for the application of the *voluntarist* method. It is the use of that method, so refined, which must be mastered, and applied, if civilization is to escape the horror which presently besieges us. In this report, I situate that voluntarist method, from the vantage-point of Leibniz's development of his notion of *monadology.*

At a time when all influential policy-shapers who are *not* philosophical voluntarists, will tend behave as bunglers, the following question is posed: *by means of what voluntarist intervention, by the rest among us, can the necessary change in direction be brought into play?*

The Problem of Historical Specificity

Whenever that discussion touches the matter of stated or implied claims to knowledge of universal principles, we should focus sharply upon a certain special problem, that of *historical specificity*. For our purposes here, we shall define and re-examine this question of historical specificity from the vantage-point of Gottfried Leibniz's notion of monadology.[12] That topic of method, so situated, is the following.

For reasons which I have defined extensively within earlier writings, any discussion of this topic, must situate itself by efficiently implied reference to the accumulation of knowledge possessed by mankind, and, more narrowly, by any specific culture, up to the time of a current discussion. In other words, the investigation of matters pertaining to the question of method set forth at the outset of this report, must adopt its empirical basis from the history of the efficient effects of the previous development of *ideas, as Plato defined the term ideas,* and *as Leibniz defined the Platonic idea of a monadology.*

Such is the setting, in which a specific culture, at a specific time, is faced with a specific challenge to its continued existence. That challenge must be seen as that culture is situated not merely within the context of the world's geography, but also the legacy of that society's cultural development, accumulated from all human history, up to that time. This retrospective view defines the broad meaning of *historical specificity.*

For example, that great artist and historian, William Shakespeare, proceeding from the legacy of England's Sir Thomas More, located the immediate historical specificity of Sixteenth-Century England in a series of historical dramas, culminating in the accession of Henry VII (Richmond) as the great reformer who created a modern England to match the model provided by the kindred, successive achievements of Jeanne d'Arc and Louis XI in France.

Thus, from that portion of Shakespeare's work, we have the unfolding of English history under the impact of imperial Venice's orchestration of the role of the Norman oligarchy throughout Europe and the Mediterranean region more broadly, over three centuries, from the time of King John I (during the time-frame of the Second through Fourth Crusades), through the Hundred Years War and the Wars of the Roses. This is a very specific chunk of English history, as also of France and of Europe and the Mediterranean region as a whole. To understand that history, we must recognize it as having a specifically coherent character, a specific character which must be brought to bear, if we are to become capable of understanding the development occurring in that setting over the sweep of centuries, and impacting

---

12. See *Gottfried Wilhelm Leibniz: Philosophical Papers and Letters*, Leroy E. Loemker, ed. (Dordrecht (Netherlands): Kluwer Academic Publishers, 1989), pp. 592-721. References are implicitly to Leibniz's *Theodicy* and posthumously published *New Essays*, the latter refuting John Locke in terms which played a decisive role in shaping the concepts and language of the 1776 U.S. Declaration of Independence. See, Philip Valenti, "The Anti-Newtonian Roots of the American Revolution," *EIR*, December 1, 1995.

relevant parts of the world, in historically specific ways, still today.

The characteristic feature of that three centuries of history, is the *relative* inevitability of such catastrophes as the mid-Fourteenth-Century New Dark Age, resulting from the defeats of the opponents of Venice's imperial maritime rule during that entire period. The Hundred Years War and the Wars of the Roses in England, represent the continuing calamity for Europe as a whole, inhering in that continued Venetian influence.[13] Thus, the coincidence of the role of Jeanne d'Arc with the preparations and outcome of the great ecumenical Council of Florence, the subsequent victory of Louis XI in France, of Henry VII in England, and the launching of the great transatlantic voyages of exploration, such as that of Christopher Columbus, which was organized by Nicholas of Cusa's circles from the great Council of Florence, typify a revolution against the evil inhering in the preceding centuries' use of Norman puppets by Venetian thalassiarchs: the Fifteenth-Century Renaissance, the revolution against the Venice legacy on which all of modern European civilization's achievements have been premised ever since.

The dramas of Friedrich Schiller, as the transmission of the heritage of Shakespeare into the German Classics, was influenced, through the work of Kästner and Lessing, represent today a still higher standard of historian's skill than Shakespeare, although both are typical of the heirs and spokesmen of the Fifteenth-Century Renaissance. Schiller's studies of the Spanish war against the Netherlands, the Thirty Years War, and of the case of Jeanne d'Arc, show the power of the great poet-historian to bring forth the essence of the true his-

EIRNS/Susan Bowen

Schiller's treatment of Joan of Arc, in his drama The Maid of Orleans, *shows the power of the great poet-historian to bring forth the essence of the true history of a people by the devices of the Classical stage.*

tory of a people by the devices of the Classical stage.

This is the same principle expressed in any performance of J.S. Bach's St. John Passion and St. Matthew Passion, which is conducted as Bach had intended the organic participation among composer, soloists, chorus, and congregation. The intention is that all, composer, soloists, chorus, and congregation, might *participate in reliving that passion within their own cognitive experiences.* Mozart's **Great Mass**, his later **Requiem**, and Beethoven's masses, express the use of art to bring about a truthful cognitive experience of the reliving of history, shared among composer, performers, and audiences. These are not fiction, not entertainments, but the adducing of the cognitive reality of history, as distinct from a reductionist's dumb reading of the shadows on the wall of a dimly firelit cave, or, as seen darkly in a mere sensory mirror of reality.[14] The superior truthfulness of great Classical art, on this account, is that it accomplishes the essential function of enabling the audiences, among others, to relive the cognitive experience of the historical subject to which the art, or an appropriate form of religious service, refers.

As I have elaborated on this point in published locations, the truthfulness of Classical artistic compositions, such as those of Shakespeare and Schiller, lies in their insight into the uses of the Classical stage, as a domain distinct from the panoramas outside. The idea presented on the Classical stage, must be a truthful representation of the idea underlying the sensory experiences of the panorama, but, the panorama and the stage are different media, differing to that effect, that, to present the idea of certain events on a vast area and lapse of time, *compactly* on the stage, the composer must, as Schiller did with the figure of Posa in **Don Carlos**, create on stage the *idea* which may not correspond ex-

---

13. By "relative inevitability," I signify the consequences inhering in stubborn adherence to a defective set of implied axiomatic beliefs and the practices associated with them.

14. *I Corinthians* 13.

actly, in every detail introduced, to the actual history, but corresponds, with historical truthfulness, to the essence of the historical reality referenced. The truth remains the same in both cases, but the media upon which the truth is staged, differ. There is no excuse, for writing tragedy as fiction, nor for interpreting Classical tragedy as the writing of fiction. Thus, no great tragedian would ever compose a work in response to some arbitrary choice of subject-matter; he would always choose a subject whose treatment was faithful to real history, and would choose only subjects for which he had first discovered a truthful representation of the real-life tragedy, a truth demonstrable, on stage, by the means available to him.

To understand the flaws and accomplishments of all Classical tragedy, from the Homeric epics through Schiller's dramas, real history must be read, and portrayed with the eyes of Plato's dialogues, as an exercise in the search for cognitive discovery of important truth.

Together with Plato's devastating moral criticism of the greatest Classical Greek tragedians before him, Schiller's historical studies, as reflected in his dramas, typify what should be understood by the term "Classical philosophy." The comparison of Schiller's treatment of Jeanne d'Arc, to Shakespeare's tragedy of Hamlet, shows that higher level in Schiller, as Plato's dialogues supersede the methods of such great artists as Aeschylus and Sophocles.

By the very nature of the subject-matter, much of the actual history of mankind in general, even our own nation, is unknown to us; however, despite that shortfall, we must and can, nonetheless, reach conclusions which have a relatively universal authority, relative to the recent millennia of the emergence and development of today's globally extended European civilization, especially six centuries of modern European civilization, and, also relative to those conclusions which have bearing on effects which might be projected for a period as long as several generations into the future.

Schiller's greatest achievement, beyond what Shakespeare accomplished at his best, lies in Schiller's degree of emphasis upon the principle of the *sublime*.[15] This distinction is shown most efficiently in his treatment of Jeanne d'Arc. Classical tragedy tends, too often, to show how a society destroys itself, often by the

deep-going moral defects of those it has chosen to place in positions of great authority, as we might be worried about the newly inaugurated President George Bush, today. That is useful, and uplifting for the audience which recognizes the possibility of a willful choice of alternative to tragedy. However, it were better to affirm the alternative, which, as in the real-life case of the Jeanne d'Arc treated by Schiller, locates the higher meaning of life and purpose of action, as in Beethoven's Opus 132 string quartet, in the sublime.

What we may claim, or might strongly suspect to have been known, from such an actual history of *ideas*, must be defined in two quite distinct, but connected categories.

In the first, straightforward case, there are some things which we can show from the past, as having been both explicitly known at that time, and can be known to us today, as either relatively valid, or clearly mistaken beliefs, as each are encountered in such specific, earlier, cultures and times. We can thus adduce corresponding, necessarily underlying assumptions of principle which are implied in the work of an historical predecessor.

Then, in the alternative, we have the muddier waters, in which the actions considered express relevant, underlying, adducible principles, which the relevant representatives may, or may not have explicitly claimed to know, or, cases in which, those who apparently claimed knowledge, left us, today, without indications of desired forms of proof which we might presently replicate.

Heraclitus & Plato, For Example

Typical of the problem of supplying presently relevant distinctions of this type, are matters posed to us by implied attributions of certain essential ontological notions, for example, to pre-Socratic thinkers such as Pythagoras, Thales, Heraclitus and their predecessors. As an illustration of that point, compare what we know of an apparent convergence between the views of Heraclitus and Plato, respectively, on this account.

For example, in the work of Plato, we encounter a definite, knowledgeable clarification of an argument, defining the essential nature of the quality of existence as *becoming*, as axiomatically, universally opposed to the reductionists' naive reading of fixed objects such as those of sense-perception. A similar argument by Heraclitus, is referenced by Plato himself, but the surviving fragments of Heraclitus's writings tease us, as if to tempt us into making extrapolations which may or may

---

15. See Friedrich Schiller, "On the Sublime," in *Friedrich Schiller, Poet of Freedom,* Vol. III, 1990, Schiller Institute, Washington, D.C., p. 255.

not be valid ones. Plato appears to admire Heraclitus' notion of becoming, but, as we may be limited to the fragments of Heraclitus more or less known to us, we can not be certain, as a matter of knowledge, that Plato's concurrence with Heraclitus on this point is thorough-going, is admissible for extrapolation of it as universal in quality. I mean, in the sense that we must attribute functional universality, to any validated *idea* defined in the strict, cognitive sense of the term *idea*.[16]

Plato's method in treating of existence as *becoming*, as implied in the famous allegory of Plato's Cave, shifts the question of the nature of existence, away from the illusory inferences of ignorant sense-certainty, up and away from what is sometimes termed "vulgar materialism." The primary empirical expression of existence, is located by Plato, where it must be situated, as *a universal ontological principle of change*, rather than those deductive, or kindred relations among the sense-certainty-like objects so greatly esteemed by the reductionists. Although Heraclitus pointed toward a similar alternative to reductionism, with his "nothing is constant but change," it is only from Plato that we first obtain the dialectical form of exposition which enables us actually *to know that principle, from a cognitive standpoint*, as a physically efficient, universal one.[17]

For example, some of the most important of the practical ideas on which the actual achievements of modern civilization depend, meet the requirements of expressing necessary ideas, but we can not show, with certainty, that the author we reference, in each case, was conscious of that implication of the way in which we may wish to adduce that idea from a modern standpoint in scientific method: as if it were an idea apprehended from a dialectical statement in terms of a *geometry of position*. That latter method, named *"Analysis Situs"* (Geometry of Situation) by Gottfried Leibniz, and known otherwise as "geometry of position,"[18] was later developed by Gauss, Abel, Riemann, et al., into the general form for expressing experimentally-defined ontological paradoxes, that, in mathematical terms, not possible within the framework of a conventionally deductive mode of mathematical argument.[19]

The distinction I am making here, is, admittedly, a fine one, but, nonetheless, like Kepler's discovery of astrophysics, in opposition to the blundering method of Copernicus, or the devastatingly infinitesimal difference between Leibniz's definition of the calculus, and the fraudulent version concocted by Leibniz-hater Leonhard Euler, Lagrange, and Cauchy, it is a crucial difference for science as a whole. Therefore, we must be certain that we understand one another clearly on this matter of seemingly fine points of distinction.

Sometimes, we know, with certainty, that the source referenced did *not* make a discovery of the form which wishful thinking might attribute to that source.[20] At other times, as in certain cases, such as Plato's reference to Heraclitus' notion of an ontological principle of universal change, we can not be certain that Heraclitus intended fully what Plato intends as the universality of an ontological principle of change; we simply lack the quality of evidence adequate to support the conclusion that Heraclitus intended the kinds of universalist implications which we can, and must adduce from Plato's conception. The need for caution in this comparison is

---

16. Autobiographically: during 1951, the puzzle posed by the similarities and differences between the import of the known fragments attributed to Heraclitus, and the clarity of Plato's argument on the ontological implications of "becoming," prompted a crucial turn, at that time, in my own approach to the problems of a science of physical economy. The qualitative differences among the Homeric outlook, the pre-Socratic thinkers, that of the Classical tragedians, and Plato's dialogues, must be appreciated if any useful knowledge for modern use is to be adduced from the study of the work of any among them. If a reader were curious as to where I developed the passion for historical specificity which I stress here, the answer is implicitly provided him in the present location.
17. See discussion of "ideas" known "from a cognitive standpoint," later in the course of these prefatory remarks. This concept of *ideas* is a central feature of all of those of my ideas which I consider important ones. It is pervasive in the writing of these pages. See, Plato, *Parmenides*.

18. Loemker, op. cit., pp. 247-248.
19. Bernhard Riemann, *"Über die Hypothesen, welche der Geometrie zu Grunde liegen,"*(1854) **Bernhard Riemanns Gesammelte Mathematische Werke**, H. Weber, ed. (New York:Dover Publications reprint edition, 1953), pp. 272-287; *"Theorie der Abel'schen Functionen,"* (1857) op. cit., pp. 88-144; and other locations, in the same collected works. It is from the standpoint of the first cited work, the 1854 habilitation dissertation, that the physical basis for Riemann's work on the implications of Abelian functions and topics of hypergeometry must be located.
20. For example, Isaac Newton did not discover a principle of universal gravitation; he produced a bungled effort to plagiarize the available, published edition of Kepler's **New Astronomy**, which Newton and his associates had available to them in England at that time. Furthermore, as Newton's three-body paradox illustrates this fact, Kepler's principle of universal gravitation can not be adduced from what Newton et al. vulgarize from their reading of Kepler as "Kepler's Three Laws." Similarly, Copernicus did not "discover" the Sun as the center of the Solar system; this was ancient Greek knowledge, long before the hoaxster Claudius Ptolemy, and was emphasized by Nicholas of Cusa during the Fifteenth Century. Kepler showed that Copernicus' method could not have produced such an conclusive, original discovery of principle.

underscored by the implications of *the historical specificity* of the lapse of time between the life of Heraclitus and the work of Plato. Similarly, in using the term "Christian platonism," we must take into account the historical specificity of the lapse of time between the death of Heraclitus and the birth of Christ.

This is a fine distinction, but not so fine that it can be competently overlooked. *It is a distinction which we must make, whenever the matter at hand involves staking the future of society upon a correct, historical appreciation of some deep universal principle*, as I am doing in these pages.

The Use of *Analysis Situs*

In such cases, where fine distinctions are obligatory, we can be certain of the author's intent, only if the author's work presents the idea in the form of the method of cognition expressed by Plato's Socratic dialogues. In modern terms, that is the method which I reference here by such terms as "*Analysis Situs*" and "geometry of position." That is the mathematical method of physical science, as opposed to the deductive, "ivory tower" constructs of the "Euclidean" geometries and related constructs of the reductionist mathematicians.

In physical science, as the example of atomic and nuclear physics underlines this fact, knowledge is never defined as empiricists and some others imply, by sense-certainty. Rather, as Plato illustrates the point by his allegory of the Cave, sense-certainty is like the irregular surface of the wall of a dimly lit cave, on which the movements of the shadows reflect real action, but do not show us directly the action itself. Thus, in physical science, we know something only to the degree we are able to demonstrate that existence of the real action, and its efficient characteristics, through experimentally verified cognitive insight. To the extent that we recognize an object solely by means of our senses, we do not actually know that object. We actually *know* only that which we know with the quality of scientific rigor, in the cognitive, anti-empiricist, anti-Kantian, way which the method of *Analysis Situs* reflects.

That dialectical method of Plato, on which Kepler and Leibniz relied, is reflected in modern scientific practice in the rigorous form identified by the terms "*Analysis Situs*" and "geometry of position." It is the method demonstrated, pervasively, in Plato's Socratic dialogues. It is the method of Carl Gauss, as Riemann, as in his 1854 habilitation dissertation, brings Gauss's work on this to general form of expression for physics

as a whole.

Rather than say, simply, "ideas," let us qualify that, by stating that I mean both the process expressed by the original discovery of an idea, and also the process of the communication of that idea, *as an idea*, from one person to another. The principles of original discovery of an idea, as typified by the original discovery of an experimentally validated universal physical principle, are identical to the means by which such an idea is communicated, as actual knowledge of that idea, from the cognitive processes of one mind, to the cognitive processes of another person.

On this account, when we use the term "idea," as Plato, Kepler, or Leibniz would, we mean, either the quality of idea associated with a universal physical principle, such as Kepler's original discovery of a principle of universal gravitation, as Kepler details this, step by step, in his ***The New Astronomy***,[21] or the idea of communication of such an idea to another individual person. Or, we mean the notion of an idea common to both such discoveries of a validated universal physical principle of non-living processes, or of living processes, and also the idea of the communication of ideas of that *specifically cognitive quality, as ideas are defined by Plato,* from one person to another.

In the first of the foregoing classes, we are pointing to ideas concerning the reciprocal relationship of the "normalized" case of the individual representative of humanity to nature. In the second class of cases, we are referring to that lawful, functional aspect of social relations (e.g., communications), in which ideas respecting either man's individual relationship to nature, or ideas of man's communication of ideas, are themselves communicated as ideas. These latter are communicated to other persons, that in the form of specifically cognitive qualities of knowledge. In the second class of cases, we should be judging such communicated ideas as in the form of hypotheses, subject to a principled form of experimental validation. The validation is defined, as to

---

21. Johannes Kepler, ***New Astronomy*** (1609), William Donahue, trans. (Cambridge: Cambridge University Press, 1992). The reader is cautioned against the hoax featured in the translator's and Owen Gingerich's fraudulent disregard for Kepler's explicit condemnation of the incompetent method employed by Claudius Ptolemy, Copernicus, and Tycho Brahe, the condemnation of those persons for a falsification of what is, in fact, what Kepler identified as the crucial characteristic of his revolutionary accomplishments in this work taken as a whole. Reading that foreword and the translator's introduction, one might imagine a detective pointing to a freshly killed body lying bloodily on the living-room floor, and the witness's responding, "I don't see any body!"

be measured in terms of society's increase of its power to exist, in and over the universe, in physical terms. Typically, this validation is to be measured per capita and per square kilometer of a normalized cross-sectional area of the Earth's surface.

In that modern case, we can say that we know the subject author's intent, because he obliges us, in that way, through that *specific faculty of cognitive insight*, to replicate the discovery of the intent of the experimentally verifiable idea in our own cognitive processes. This principle governs the way in which communication of ideas, as Plato defines *ideas*, occurs among living persons; it is also the way in which ideas are communicated, as *ideas*, from the past to the present, and to the future.

In opposition to that single step of perception, through which we learn to recognize objects in the form of sense-perceptions (e.g., the empiricist's brutish notion of "sense certainty"), the individual act of knowing an *idea* requires three steps. First, there must be the recognition of a true paradox of an ontological form, in judging observed phenomena from the standpoint of what were previously considered universally valid ways of interpreting such apparent types of phenomena.[22] Second, there must be an act of *hypothetical* discovery of some universally efficient principle, a discovery which solves the paradox. Third, there must be an experimental test of the discovery. That must be a test designed, not merely to show that the hypothetical principle works in some cases, but must work as an integral part of knowledge as a whole. In other words, the test must show that the hypothetical principle is either universal, or not. If not, it is not a principle.[23]

Since the first and third steps are both demonstrated experimentally, a second person who repeats those steps recognizes the successful nature of the thought which engendered the hypothetical discovery in the mind of the original discoverer, as recreated in his own.

It is in that way, that the imperceptible is known, because the existence of that idea is efficient in controlling the shadows on the wall of Plato's Cave. This sharing of the act of discovery of an experimentally validated principle, defines an *idea* of the Platonic type. Ideas of principle generated and validated in this way, thus represent communicable, and also efficient ideas for practice, even though the idea itself is not visible to the mere senses.

Thus, the subject of history, properly apprehended, is the history of ideas, as that is to be defined in the terms which I have just summarized. Thus, the only valid idea of history, is the history of ideas.

In *Analysis Situs,* the evidence of a contradiction is stated within the terms of a pre-existing, referenced set of ideas of principle. Such a set of ideas might be the notion of the physical universe consistent with a so-called Euclidean model, as in the case of the paradox which prompted Fermat to discover a principle of quickest time governing the propagation of light. By stating the case for reflection, as in contrast to the case for refraction, Fermat defined an ontological paradox existing within the so-called Euclidean domain of then widely-taught ideas of the physical universe. The experimental validation of Fermat's discovery, as by Huyghens, and by the anti-Newtonians Leibniz, Bernouilli, and Fresnel later, defined the principle of universal least action as not merely an hypothesis, but a validated idea corresponding to a universal physical principle.

Thus, to summarize what I have just said:

In all cases, the efficient generation and communication of ideas occurs, as I shall show at a later point in this report, solely in the paradoxical form of *Analysis Situs,* or *geometry of position,* each mutually contradictory pair of elements of which, expresses the typically underlying form of crucial statements of a Socratic dialogue. For the simplest valid classroom presentation of the point, consider again Fermat's contrast of reflection to refraction, as a paradox which defines a universal principle of quickest time, as superseding the mistaken conception of shortest distance. This is a typical example, as a statement, of the way in which a validatable discovery of universal principle is generated, by stating the relevant paradox in the form of geometry of position.

The communication of an idea occurs in the same, three-step way just summarized.

This explicitly Platonic dialectical method, as em-

---

22. The same function is performed in Classical poetry, and in literate forms of written and spoken speech, by irony in general, and metaphor in particular. Notable is Galileo-trained Thomas Hobbes' hatred of metaphor. Metaphor, which is the literary expression of the same principle as *Analysis Situs,* is the use of language in which cognition is expressed. Since Hobbes, in the footsteps of Galileo's master Paolo Sarpi, is committed to denying the cognitive nature of the human individual personality, as distinct from the beasts, he, like his professed admirer and follower Henry A. Kissinger (op. cit.), is obliged, by his hatred of both man and reason, to demand the exclusion of human behavior from the composing of literature.

23. This is sometimes known as the principle of "unique experiment."

ployed by such as Plato, Nicholas of Cusa,[24] Kepler, Leibniz, and Riemann, is, contrary to the hoaxster G.W.F. Hegel, et al., the only meaningful use of the term "dialectical method." This is the method by which all discoveries of validatable ideas are prompted, and the basis for the design of experiments which test the universality of the hypothetical principles generated within the mind by the prompting statement of an ontological paradox in the form of geometry of position.

These ideas are not images of sense-perception, but experimentally demonstrated discoveries of solutions for paradoxes which inhere in the flawed nature of sense-certainty as such. The discovery of principles, beyond the reach of sense-perception, in the domain of microphysics, typifies the notion of experimentally validatable ideas of universal physical principle, which are prompted by paradoxes which have been presented in the rigorous form of statement required by geometry of position. Max Planck's definition of the quantum of action, typifies this, as does his defense of scientific method against the fanatical followers of the positivist Ernst Mach.

It is the discovery and experimental validation of those ideas, beyond sense-certainty, generated by the prompting action of a paradox stated in the form of geometry of position, which we are able to recognize as *knowledge*, as the strictly defined use of that term, knowledge, is to be distinguished from both merely fantastic illusions, such as symbolism, and naive interpretations of literal sense-perception. It is only such ideas, so defined, which constitute *knowledge*, as distinct from *mere learning*.

Courtesy AIP Niels Bohr Library

Max Planck (1858-1947). His definition of the quantum of action, and his defense of scientific method against the positivists, typify experimentally validatable ideas of universal physical principle, which are prompted by paradoxes which have been presented in the rigorous form of statement required by geometry of position.

---

24. In the founding of modern experimental physical science, in Cusa's **De Docta Ignorantia**, the point of origin of the work of Luca Pacioli, Leonardo da Vinci, William Gilbert, and Johannes Kepler, and such as Leibniz, Gauss, and Riemann after them. This method was known, as during the Sixteenth Century, as the Socratic method of *docta ignorantia*.

How To Use History

Even in the case, in which the replication of a relevant physical experiment, demonstrates, dialectically, the feasibility of the application specified by an author, if we lack access to a specified cognitive exercise, as might have been provided by the referenced source, we are left with a certain degree of uncertainty respecting that source's intent. By observation, we might conclude that the result is a plausible one, on the surface; but, we do not recognize the way in which the author reached that conclusion. In other words, we witness the result, but we do not actually *know* the process, *from that source*, by which the supposed discovery of the result was accomplished.

In other words, the minds of discoverers from the past are able to communicate with our minds, even if that discoverer were long deceased, through the three-step method outlined above. So, we, too, are empowered to communicate to the minds of persons who will be conceived and born long after we are dead. This relationship, defined in terms of ideas, among past, present, and future, is the equivalence of the idea of history to the history of ideas. It is not through learning rooted in sense-certainty, but only through the cognitive communication of *ideas* of a Platonic quality, that we are in efficient relationship to humanity as a whole, to our predecessors, our contemporaries, and our posterity alike.

This carries us a very important step, above and beyond the elementary, three-step process of discovery and communication summarized above. When we act as individual cognitive beings, rather than like beasts, rutting like pigs in the trough of sense-certainty, the powers of cognition which we bring to bear upon anything like an ontological paradox, reflect the full weight of our individual cognitive experience of previous generations, implicitly all humanity which has existed to date. So, the mere existence of the development of language typifies such a cumulative impact of the cognitive experience of the past upon the individual in the present.

This points to the indispensable role of a Classical-humanist mode of universal primary and secondary education for all members of our society. The primary goal and function of education, must be to enable the young, in particular, to relive the important cognitive experiences of past generations, especially the great discoveries and the great crises of earlier cultures and peoples. It is in the seeking of cognitive truth, in such Classical-humanist modes of education of the young in ideas, that education provides a foundation for the moral development of the character of the young person, and, hence, also the adult.

The superior moral character of the individual enjoying the benefits of a Classical-humanist education, in contrast to today's more popular practices, expresses itself not only in the development of persons who are usually more moral, more sane than in other parts of the population, but endowed with superior qualities of intellectual achievement in whatever profession takes them up. Thus, the idea of an historically so-defined generality of cognitive development, points to an induced state of mind described as the expression of a principle of higher hypothesis, expressed, typically, as the individual's power to generate entire families of discoveries.

Thus, in the cases in which our access to the intent of reported ideas is not in the form suited to cognitive communication of past with present generations, we can not be confident that we actually know the idea of that earlier generation merely from the facts transmitted to us. Where such doubt arises, we can neither claim that that author's intent in the matter corresponds to our own cognitive insight into the matter, nor, as in the referenced case of Heraclitus, can we disregard the efficiency of the experimental evidence which might support that author's pertinent, apparent conclusion. We could never understand history, and the making of history, until we have adduced the reliable principles involved in such crucial cases of shadings of difference in interpretation.

We can not ignore the influence of apparent ideas of principle, even in the case we remain uncertain as to whether or not a certain people understood efficiently the idea by which their shaping of their history was influenced. Even provably false ideas, if they command that practical relevance, such as the provably false and poisonous notions of empiricism, can not be ignored,

but must be given critical consideration, if not implicit trust, in our accounts.

Thus, in our efforts to account for what we presently know, from our familiarity with some relevant aspects of the earlier existence of mankind, we actually know, chiefly, only certain slices from that relatively tiny span of human existence which we study as that portion coinciding with so-called recorded history. Even from much of that record, our available evidence is fragmentary and otherwise imperfect.

On account of such imperfections in the record available to us, we must pay special attention to the possible implications of what we do not know, and also to those border-areas, in which our knowledge is imperfect, as in such cases from Greek history as Pythagoras, Thales, and Heraclitus. The achievement of the degree of rigor we must apply, to be justified in stating, "I know," depends upon our sensitivity to the possible implications of that which we do not know.

This precaution, as it applies to study of the past, is the indispensable training of the mind in the kind of discipline required for work in areas in which history has yet to come into existence, in the effort to present reasonable forecasts of the future. Without this rigor, we could not trust our estimates of the consequences of the choices of change in axioms we are considering for implementation.

Therefore, it is only through acquiring the habit of studying history as the cognitive history of the production of ideas, that we might develop what is best labelled an epistemological sense about ideas. It is when the term "philosophy" is used to point toward a matured, richly developed "epistemological sense" of history, as the history of ideas, that the competent forecaster emerges.

On that account, there is little that pleases certain epistemologically matured discoverers more, than to discover that turning up the kind of evidence from what had been previously considered to be unknown patches in history, which shows that one was right, or wrong, in his attitude toward the possible significance of topical areas in which he had previously lacked knowledge. In science, we must make great leaps into the realm of the hypothetical; but, those leaps are permitted only to the degree we are epistemologically circumspect respecting opinions in areas from both past and future history, yet unexplored, as I have illustrated this warning in the foregoing remarks on the exemplary case from Heraclitus's fragments. You shall discover below, why I place that repeated emphasis on that illustration.

With the modern followers of Plato, Nicholas of Cusa, Leonardo da Vinci, Kepler, Leibniz, Gauss, and Riemann, most notably, modern science is defined as a realm, in which the matter of the author's conscious intent to claim a universal principle, is made known to us through the author's reliance on experimental modes of demonstration of what are claimed as discovered universal principles. All topics within this specific realm, are immediately situated within the bounds defined by Plato's work; on this account, we can not disregard relevant work which preceded that of Plato, but neither can we be certain that Plato's predecessors saw these matters as we are able to adduce the clear intention of Plato and his indicated modern followers. Plato's explicit reference to Heraclitus is a model case in point.

Before turning to the subject of the monadology itself, conclude this introductory section of the report with the following summary of the most crucial points we have presented thus far. To summarize that experimental method to which we have referred here, we have the following.

Discovery of a valid universal physical principle, begins with a set of facts recognized as as an ontological paradox. Such an *ontological paradox* must be, then, rigorously restated, in a mathematical or quasi-mathematical form, exactly as Fermat showed the paradoxical relationship between reflection and refraction. From this paradox, Fermat adduced a universal principle of quickest action, rather than shortest-distance for refraction of light.

Thus, prompted by the combined impact of Kepler's discovery of a principle of universal gravitation, and Fermat's principle, Huyghens, Leibniz et al., proceeded, through a series of relevant, well-crafted experimental designs, to Leibniz's development of the original differential calculus, and to his later formulation of a general principle of universal least action. It was the latter formulation which led him directly, to his most crucial contribution to physical science, his monadology.[25]

So, I went from defending Leibniz's monadology, against Kant, during my adolescence, to my discoveries of the 1948-1952 interval, to Riemann. From there, I went to the "pre-Socratics" and Plato, and on from there, back to Plato and Leonardo da Vinci, and, thence,

back to Nicholas of Cusa! So, I, too, like Leibniz, after Fermat and Huyghens, traversed the ironical pathway of the quickest time.

2. Monadology

The philosophically *voluntarist* method by which individuals might willfully bring about axiomatic changes in the direction of future human history, can not be efficiently defined as an undertaking, except from the standpoint implicit in Leibniz's discovery of a *monadology*.

At this point, we must confront a problem, concerning the relationship between mathematics and physical science. Most modern university graduates in mathematics have, so to speak, stumbled and broken their intellectual legs, over this problem. The reason for those failures, is not that the subject of geometry, as we have to consider it here, is so terribly complicated. The problem is the impossibility of understanding what is actually an elementary proposition, which I am about to address here, without asking the reader to give up a certain commonplace prejudice, which spills over from the day-to-day beliefs of ignorant people into the secondary and university classroom, still today. To continue with our presentation, we must, at this point, pause amid the argument I have been developing, to make clear what is actually meant by so-called Riemannian geometry.

Prior to the introduction of the institution of the modern sovereign nation-state, which was first established during the course of Europe's Fifteenth-Century, Italy-centered Renaissance, all known forms of society treated the majority of mankind as human cattle, hunted, or used, herded, and culled, like beasts, that by ruling castes and their armed and other classes of lackeys. This form of society was known as *the oligarchical model* of Babylon. Such was the tradition of ancient Babylon, the Sparta of the Delphi cult of the Pythian Apollo, ancient Rome, and feudalism under the hegemony of the combined forces of the imperial maritime power of Venice and its Norman allies.

This model was directly contrary to Christian belief. It was a violation of the Christian definition of human nature; but it persisted, nonetheless. It was not until the period of the great ecumenical Council of Florence and its aftermath in Louis XI's France and Henry VII's England, that the anti-oligarchical principle of the *general*

---

25. See note 2.

welfare, or *common good*, was introduced as a condition for the legitimacy of government. The history of globally extended modern European civilization, since that time, has been a continuing conflict between the persistence of the old oligarchical model, as typified by the British monarchy, and the sovereign nation-state, as typified by the British monarchy's leading adversary, the American intellectual tradition. Every major war within European civilization since the Fifteenth Century, including the religious wars of the interval 1511-1648, has been an expression of the efforts of the oligarchical faction to stamp out the existence of the sovereign nation-state and the principles of economy associated with that nation-state model.

This principle of the general welfare, first introduced to government during the Fifteenth-Century Renaissance, is that expressed by the 1776 U.S. Declaration of Independence and the Preamble of the 1789 Federal Constitution. The typification of those principles of economy of a sovereign nation-state, is the anti-"free trade," so-called American System of political-economy, as most widely recognized in connection with the names of Treasury Secretary Alexander Hamilton, Friedrich List, and Henry C. Carey.

The cases of France's Dr. François Quesnay, Lord Shelburne's lackey Adam Smith, and Immanuel Kant, are typical expressions of the kind of ideologies which the oligarchical faction has thrown up, in its attempted ideological counterattacks against the influence of the emergence of the modern sovereign nation-state. That is a problem whose typical effects are to be addressed, as a crucial interpolation, at this point of the report. Although man is naturally endowed with those creative powers of reason, cognition, which set man apart from and above the beasts, and although this principle of cognition is characteristic of Christian belief, as *I Corinthians* 13 and other sources emphasize, feudal society and its legacies sought to suppress those forms of cultural development which did not abort the development of the cognitive powers of the individual human mind.

That same anti-Christian campaign by European civilization's oligarchical interests, has been often conducted through the use of pseudo-Christian cults. Such was the tradition of the slaveholder class in the relevant Southern U.S. states; such were the dogmas of economic and social policy of the Physiocrats and Shelburne's Adam Smith; such was the central feature of the argument made by Leibniz-hating, pro-irrationalist

Self-anointed Pontifex Maximus, Louis XIV. In the tradition of the pagan Louis, François Quesnay preached that the wealth of the feudal estates were a product of the landlord's aristocratic title to that land, and the peasants on the estate merely cattle whose labor made no contribution to the gain of output over costs.

Imannuel Kant, on behalf of the anti-Classical German Romantic movement of the late Eighteenth and Nineteenth centuries. Such was the Romantic, irrationalist basis for Nazi doctrine, for example.

Take Quesnay's Physiocratic doctrine of *laissez-faire*, for example. Quesnay, whose ideology was in the tradition of the notorious, pro-feudalist, Norman *Fronde* and the legacy of the pagan worship of the Delphic Apollo under France's self-anointed *Pontifex Maximus*, King Louis XIV, preached that the wealth of the feudal estates were a product of the landlord's aristocratic title to that land, and the peasants on the estate merely cattle whose labor made no contribution to the gain of output over costs. Adam Smith's doctrine of "free trade," which was chiefly a plagiarism of the doctrine of Quesnay and other French Physiocrats of that time, makes the same argument. Such was the doctrine of John Locke, whose teaching, under the rubrics "Life, Liberty, and Property," was the fundamental law of the Constitution of Confederate States of America, and the basis in taught slaveholders' law for the maintenance of the system of chattel slavery, and prohibition against allowing literacy to "those of African descent," under the Confederacy and its tradition since, to the present day.

A Ku Klux Klan rally in Savannah, Georgia. The KKK, sponsored by President Woodrow Wilson, typifies the "Christian fundamentalism" of one grouping of pseudo-Christians, the "religious beliefs of those who are proud to consider themselves human cattle."

Among the victims of such pro-oligarchical teachings and practices, the serf-holders, slaveholders, and their like fostered a curious form of pseudo-Christian belief, sometimes called "Christian fundamentalism," which was spread throughout much of what is called "The Bible Belt" today. Call it the "religious beliefs of those who are proud to consider themselves human cattle." Consistently, the sundry varieties of this pseudo-Christian belief, with their notorious "single issue" style in grievances, were often lumped together under the rubric of the lowest of the "low church" cults, as the so-called Pentacostalists typify the more extremely irrationalist examples of this. Not surprisingly, the hard core of those "low church" fanatics is found in the same localities of the U.S.A. in which President Woodrow Wilson's sponsorship of the revival of the Ku Klux Klan (KKK), and the influence of the so-called Nashville Agrarians, have been spread inside the U.S.A. during the course of the Twentieth Century.

These populist varieties of religious cults, and their echoes into secular society, are found typically among those unfortunates who view themselves, in practice, as an underclass, that of virtual human cattle. By the so-called "logic" of reaction-formation, they made a god in their own image, a god made in the image, not of man, but of human cattle, or the "golden calf."

As the spread of the policies associated with Nixon's Southern Strategy campaign of 1966-1968, turned the formerly industrialized regions of the U.S., on which the nation's prosperity chiefly depended, into what became known as a "rust belt," and as the skill-levels of employees, and number of jobs held, and hours worked or spent in commuting increased, the emphasis upon cognitive self-development in personal and family life dwindled, increasing thus the ration of the total labor-force which viewed its virtually unchangeable condition as that of almost slave-like human cattle, like the Southern "poor whites" under the rule of those slaveholders in whose interest the Confederacy was established.

As trends in popular culture, so called, plunged downward, during the recent thirty-five years, the almost brainless irrationalism of the lowest of the low-church types, the most human-cattle-like types, spread and worsened. The result of that has been the reaction-formation in which our nation's life is polluted, more and more, by those religious and kindred expressions of anti-cognitive irrationalism typified by the lowest of the low-church cults, such as those of Rev. Pat Robertson and Rev. Jerry Falwell. This trend is complemented by the soaring incidence of mental disorders within the population as a whole.

The result is, inevitably, both the spread of pseudo-Christian cults, echoing the Flagellant hordes of Europe's Fourteenth Century, and a growing hostility to everything rational in science and culture generally. The result has been, as in the moral and intellectual degeneration of Eighteenth-Century England under the House of Hanover, the transformation of a large and growing ration of our population into "Yahoos."

The popular ignorant prejudices among the victims of that populist disorder, read matters of science as curious religious sects usually misread the Bible. The ignorant populist insists that "God wrote the Bible so that

Our nation's life has become polluted, more and more, by anti-cognitive irrationalism, typified by the lowest of the low-church cults, such as those of Rev. Pat Robertson (left) and Rev. Jerry Falwell.

ignorant people like me" ("human cattle") would automatically have a perfect understanding of what is written in the translation "which we use in our church." They believe that everything can be explained in terms of simple sense-perceptions, and that this means that all objects perceived by their senses are floating about, moving in a kind of infinite "soup," of empty space, which has four, mutually independent senses of direction: up, down, sideways, and time. They believe that each of these senses of direction is infinite in length. In other words, today's populist varieties of religious belief are fairly described as either "Religion for Dummies," or, simply, "religion suited for the beliefs of those proud to be human cattle."

For that reason, if we put aside some of their wild-eyed notions about such exotic matters as "Bible prophecy," they believe in statistics and, therefore, in luck (e.g., gambling, mutual funds, etc.). Their idea of statistics, is based on the assumption that God designed the universe in such a way that it could be perfectly understood by dummies: everything one needs to know, can be discovered and proven by seeing, hearing, smelling, and touching. From the sermons in their churches, and their prayers, we observe a religion centered upon bargaining, at God's back-door, for personal favors, chiefly in matters of health, sexual gratification, and wealth. Their religion reminds us of dutiful slaves begging for

hand-outs at the back door of the master's big white house. They believe that everything that the human senses can observe, can be understood by drawing more or less straight lines among dots on paper.

Put the son or daughter of such a populist type in school, and the student's family background will have prepared that student to accept the beliefs of Seventeenth-Century ideological types known as "empiricists," such as Galileo Galilei, Thomas Hobbes, Rene Descartes, John Locke, and Isaac Newton. In short, their ideas of physics are based on what is often called a "Euclidean" model of space, time, and matter. Their religious-like family traditions cause them to reject any idea about the real world which is not consistent with the empiricist's pro-oligarchical doctrine of "God for Dummies."

It happens, of course, that the real world does not work in the way that so-called "Euclidean model" requires. Unfortunately, often, the mass of evidence which proves that the world does not work that way, does not convince the believing populist to give up his unworkable model of reality. Instead, he or she adopts, even invents superstitions, which pretend to explain away the evidence that the "Euclidean model" does not work, and places his confidence in a form of prayer which does not differ from black magic, turning to witchcraft, in the effort to compel a deity to bestow upon him benefits which reason and reality would never allow.

As a expression of the popularity of those superstitions, university students have often heard the professor instructing students to the following effect.

"Euclidean geometry is the logical form for the application of mathematics to describing of physical phenomena. This geometry consists of a collection of self-evident definitions, axioms, and postulates, all of which are given to us by a

The populists believe in statistics, and therefore in luck (e.g., gambling). Their idea of statistics, is based on the assumption that God designed the universe in such a way that it could be perfectly understood by dummies: everything one needs to know, can be discovered and proven by seeing, hearing, smelling, and touching.

purely intuitive interpretation of nature and its phenomena."[26]

The fraud in that professor's argument, is identified most efficiently, by pointing out that he pretends that the paradox of Plato's Cave never existed.

His geometric model (or its algebraic parody) assumes that cause and effect move between points along straight lines, pretty much in the same way as the usual financial accountant argues that *profit* is *income* less *costs and expenses*, instead of the more sensible approach, of considering the *physical actions reflected as some* costs and expenses as the causes of both income and profits, and attempting to discover which of them does what. Worse, the accountant who reads his accounts all too literally for his client's good, will regard as a profitable "cost-saving," the elimination of expenditures on which the continued maintenance and improvement of output and profitability depend—as "de-

regulation" has done to many sectors of the U.S. economy, in such a devastating degree, especially during the recent quarter-century since the inauguration of President Jimmy Carter.

In a real economy, the increase of output over the costs and expenses incurred to produce that output, is the result of the application of *physical action* to the process by which the output is produced and distributed. These actions express physical principles, most of which can not be competently represented in so-called "Euclidean," or analogous arithmetic or algebraic terms.

In real economy, contrary to such pseudo-economists of the stopped-up kitchen-sink-drain variety as Senator Phil Gramm, economy means, essentially, physical economy. Physical economy, my specialty, is the discovery of physical principles and the technologies derived from those discoveries, which enable mankind to produce an output in excess of the *physical* cost of the efforts required for that production. What is shown on the wall of the financial accountant's dimly lit cave, are only the shadows of the reality which the all-too-typical financial accountant, by choice of profession, and by affinity for the class of dangerous lunatics known as monetarists, refuses to see.

For that reason, all real physical science is axiomatically non-Euclidean, and not a matter of a formalist interpretation of the "postulate of parallels." This does not mean that the Nineteenth-Century treatment of the matter of parallels, as by Janos Bolyai and Lobatchevsky, was not useful. These discussions are to be viewed as scrutiny of propositions stated in the form of *Analysis Situs,* in the same sense as Fermat's overturning the fallacy of assuming that light follows always the shortest pathway, instead of the quickest pathway, which may not be the shortest distance.

It is always through the exhaustive exploration of paradoxes, such as the paradoxes of the attempt to prove the existence of a parallel postulate, that the alert, cognitive mind is prompted to discover higher principles which overturn all of the intuitive assumptions of

---

26. Even worse than this "Euclidean" dogma, is the case in which the professor and his textbook fly from geometry into a more or less purely abstract algebra, or arithmetic, which contains all of the foolishness of the "Euclidean geometric" view, but does not remove the "Euclidean" dogma's flaws, but merely hides them from view, as Bertrand Russell acolytes such as Norbert Wiener ("Cybernetics") and John von Neumann ("systems analysis") did.

what is still today, prevalent guises for generally accepted classroom varieties of mathematical physics. Critical treatments of the "parallel postulate," were neither the meal, nor the fuel by which it was cooked; those treatments were the oven in which the cooks were attempting to test the recipes with which they were experimenting.

The confusion over "non-Euclidean" geometries arises, only when the mathematician gets no further than developing a statement in the form of *Analysis Situs,* and never reaches the next step, as Riemann did, of discovering the geometry which replaces entirely the paradox-ridden debris of so-called "Euclidean" geometry's cultish application to physics. Typical of the incompetents, are those who attempt to compare Riemann's habilitation dissertation to some aspect of the discussion of the parallel postulate by others. *With Riemann's approach, the parallel postulate, as such, enters nowhere in the formulation of the design.*

The Riemannian solution is resisted, chiefly, because the empiricists, who dominate the academic classroom still today, usually refuse to allow anything on campus which might prove offensive to those same, populist traditions which I have identified as also turning up prominently in the heathen delusions expressed as "Religion for Dummies."

In real science, formal, intuitive classroom mathematics is left behind. All intuitive forms of definitions, axioms, and postulates are discarded, simply because they are intuitive, rather than being the required universal principles, validated as such by appropriate qualities of experiment. Therefore, put aside the mathematics of "Religion for Dummies," and adopt instead, the notions of physical geometry consistent with the crucial experimental evidence.

The pivotal feature of the argument to this effect, involves the implications of Leibniz's notion of *characteristics*, as, about a century and a half later, Riemann employed that conception as central to his habilitation dissertation.[27] Leibniz's notion of such characteristics, on which his definition of the differential of the calculus was premised, reflected Kepler's proof of the incompetence of the method employed by Copernicus, Tycho Brahe, and others, and also reflected the development of the notion of quickest time as introduced by Fermat.

Thus, Riemann's work implicitly defines the essential feature of the existence of a distinct *natural object*, as Vernadsky defines a "natural object,"[28] by its characteristic, as Kepler defines a planetary orbit as a characteristic. So, the differential of the Leibniz calculus (contrary to the Euler-Cauchy hoax commonly taught in universities today) is, from the standpoint of "ivory tower" mathematics, an axiomatically incommensurable magnitude, comparable to the distinctiveness of the unique characteristic of a specific Keplerian planetary orbit.

Here lies the difference between physical science taught as mathematics-at-the-blackboard, and real physical science: as Riemann emphasizes that crucial distinction in the concluding portion of his habilitation dissertation. This is the crucial argument already made by Kepler, against the connect-the-dots method of Ptolemy, Copernicus, and Tycho Brahe, in his ***New Astronomy***. It is the crucial difference between the competent physics of Leibniz's definition of the calculus, and the fraudulent alternations in that calculus made by the "ivory tower" ideologues Euler, Cauchy, et al. The existence of different natural objects in the universe, each with distinct characteristic, including the human mind, defines a *monad*. Hence, Leibniz's *monadology*. Hence, Riemann's leading contributions to physical science.

Therefore, the first step now to be taken, is to situate that topic of monadology in the form relevant to that specific argument.

In forecasting the results of man's efforts to will-

---

27. Cf. Riemann, habilitation dissertation, Sec.III, op. cit., pp.283-288. Anyone who has examined Riemann's work more closely, and taken into account the political situation in post-Carlsbad Decrees Germany at that time, will recognize the references to Archimedes, Galileo, and Newton, in this dissertation, as politically dictated references to a a Galileo and Newton, whom Riemann already regarded at that time as little better than hoaxsters.

28. See, Vladimir I. Vernadsky, *"On the Fundamental Material-energetic Difference between Living and Non-Living Natural Bodies in the Biosphere"* (1938), Jonathan Tennenbaum and Rachel Douglas, trans., ***21st Century Science & Technology***, Winter 2000-2001. This was the first full translation into English of this crucial 1938 paper by Vernadsky, offering the best insight into a body of ideas otherwise known from the work of the great founder of biogeochemistry. It was earlier work of Vernadsky, along the same lines, but less thorough than the 1938 piece referenced here, which I employed, in Spring 1973, as part of the core argument for a science of physical economy, upon which the subsequent founding of the Fusion Energy Foundation (FEF) and its influential ***Fusion*** magazine, was premised. For a recent biography of Vernadsky, see Kendall E. Bailes, ***Science and Russian Culture in An Age of Revolutions: V.I. Vernadsky and His Scientific School, 1863-1945*** (Bloomington: Indiana University Press, 1990).

fully change his future, we encounter two connected classes of challenge.

The first challenge, is to discover how man exerts control over nature, to the effect of maintaining and improving man's ability to maintain the numbers and quality of life of our species' existence. In the science of physical economy, we measure the result in terms of changes in demographic characteristics of both entire populations and typical households, and per capita and per square kilometer of our planet's normalized surface-area. We emphasize those ideas, both ideas of physical principles of non-living processes, and those of living processes, through which increased mastery of the universe, per capita, is effected on behalf of our species.

In this first case, therefore, we are estimating a normalized expression of man's per-capita relationship to nature, a relationship expressed as a function of ideas.

The second challenge, is to define those principles of social relations, by means of which, ideas of the first class are transmitted to the effect of enabling society to coordinate its efforts for effective use of principles through which man's increased power, per capita, in and over nature, is accomplished. These principles are exemplified by the principles of invention and performance of Classical artistic compositions in plastic and non-plastic forms, and in the application of the same Classical artistic principles to the comprehension of history and statecraft.

The two sets of conceptions, taken today, represent the development of the human intellect, as a Classical-humanist form of education best serves that end.

Now, consider examples of the first of the two classes of discoveries.

What Are Physical Principles?

Taking into account all the relevant matter that is to be considered here today, we have included, for special consideration, a comprehensive form of modern mathematical physics, which was begun with the crucial discoveries made by the founder of that branch of science, Johannes Kepler. The pivot of Kepler's most crucial discovery, was his discrediting of that childish, connect-the-dots methods commonly employed by the malicious Romantic hoaxster Claudius Ptolemy, and also by the well-meaning, but systemically erring Copernicus and Tycho Brahe.

By recognizing the Platonic implications of the paradoxical curvature of the orbit of the planet Mars, to-

EIRNS/Christopher Lewis

Johannes Kepler (1571-1630) freed science from the suffocating grip of "ivory tower" varieties of mathematics, and located the identity of a planetary orbit in a characteristically incommensurable value corresponding to a universal principle of harmonics, that is specific to an orbit which is not necessarily of uniform curvature.

gether with related evidence, Kepler freed science from the suffocating grip of "ivory tower" varieties of mathematics, and located the identity of a planetary orbit in a characteristically incommensurable value corresponding to a universal principle of harmonics, that specific to an orbit which is not necessarily of uniform curvature. In other words, Kepler defined the orbit as measured in terms of a constant, but not necessarily uniformly curved, but measurable effect of *Platonic* change.

He met that challenge of the individual orbit, by defining the Solar system, considered, functionally, as an harmonically unified whole, as a subsuming, (in Riemann's terms:) *multiply-connected manifold* of such change. So, Kepler was first to discover, thus, that principle of universal gravitation which would-be plagiarizers intellectually crippled by the influence of empiricism, such as Isaac Newton, could never even begin to grasp as a cognitive conception of principle. [29]

So, Kepler's founding of the first competent form of modern astrophysics, defined certain crucial problems of universal physics, which he relegated to the attentions of future mathematicians. When Kepler's such discoveries were matched with Fermat's discovery of an "anti-Euclidean" geometrical principle of quickest time, as in paradoxical contradiction of the so-called "Euclidean" notion of shortest distance, a generalized form of development of modern physical science, was set into motion, by such followers of Nicholas of Cusa, Leonardo da Vinci, and Kepler, as Christiaan Huyghens and Gottfried Leibniz.

On this basis, Leibniz developed the original differential and integral calculus, according to the combined prescriptions and implications of Kepler's and Fermat's seminal discoveries. This calculus is to be contrasted with the fraudulent, but popularized classroom definitions, as the latter are supplied, with the mere appearance of the Leibniz calculus, by such malicious figures as Leibniz-hater Euler, Euler's follower Lagrange, and the plagiarizing (e.g., of Abel) hoaxster and Laplace creature Cauchy.

Out of Leibniz's accomplishments in this direction, came his discovery of a principle of *universal least action*, and the still higher principle known as his *monadology*. Through the work of, chiefly Kästner and his student Gauss, and with important contributions by Monge, Carnot, et al., we have the crucial and unique contributions to the founding of a true and comprehensive anti-Euclidean geometry by Bernhard Riemann.

Riemann's 1854 habilitation dissertation, marks the

first act freeing physical science completely, and mathematics, too, from the grip of those "ivory tower" fantasies which had crippled, more or less severely, most of modern scientific work up to that time. This accomplishment, by Riemann, provides the Gaussian foundations for the development of my view of what Vladimir Vernadsky defined as the *noösphere*.[30] It is my situating that notion of the noösphere within the framework of my own discoveries in the field of a science of physical economy, that the connection of Leibniz's principle of *monadology* to solving that problem of *voluntarism* set forth here, can be rendered more fully comprehensible today.

I situate this latter subject by summarizing, as follows, what I have described in earlier locations, as those implications of the concept of noösphere which are brought into their necessary focus by my work in physical economy.

> 1. *By a physical principle, I signify an experimentally validatable, discovered principle, whose application generates a human effect within, and upon the universe, a quality of effect not otherwise predetermined, than by the impact of the willful human application of that discovery of a universal physical principle.*

The specific quality of difference between that, my preceding definition of universal physical principle, and the usual classroom definitions, is more easily recognized by reference to Vernadsky's definition of the noösphere.

Already, as in 1938, Vernadsky supplied a rigorous definition of the noösphere. The human *noëtic* will,[31] transforms the functionally definable relationship of the biosphere to the universe it both inhabits and reshapes. The question left unanswered by Vernadsky, is what function defines the way in which mankind may acquire *foreknowledge* of how to take the next step in transforming mankind's action on the pre-existing noösphere?

This is a proposition of the same general type, as Kepler's response to the evident non-uniformity of the curvature of planetary orbits. Where does the determining *intention* lie, by means of which the present moment of action already contains the immediate next turn in a trajectory of not necessarily uniform curvature? This

---

29. See Kepler, ***The Harmony of the World***, E.J. Aiton, A.M. Duncan, and J.V. Field, trans. (The American Philosophical Society: 1997), passim. Note the way in which the "equal areas" phenomon is applied to the distinction of the relative values among the characteristics of the various orbits. This is the root of the way in which Newton, et al., formally incurred the "three-body paradox." It is the exclusion of Kepler's emphasis on the crucial principle of harmonics, from the Newtonians' bowdlerization of Kepler's work, which leads the Newtonians and the credulous fools who follow them, into the pits of the "three-body problem." To attempt to separate the well-tempered harmonics embedded in Kepler's treatment of "equal areas," must necessarily create the "three-body paradox" in elementary classroom physics, as it tends to foster bad musical composition and interpretation among the Romantics. In noting the general case of hysterical denial of such a connection by the Newton devotees generally, note the exemplary relevance of the hysterical denial of such a connection in Kepler's astrophysics, over which H. Helmholtz and his accomplice Ellis had their fits (***Sensations of Tone***) against J.S. Bach et al., on the subjects of *bel canto* voice-training and on the related matters of well-tempering. This and related implications of the connection between the work of Kepler and that of Bach, is a special topic of historiography in itself.

---

30. Op. cit.

31. Hence, Vernadsky termed the result a *noösphere*.

was, contrary to Euler and Cauchy, Leibniz's requirement for the "infinitesimal" interval of the differential calculus. In Kepler's usage: how do we define the *Mind* of the planet; how do we define that stubbornly persisting expression of the *intention* of the planet which can not be attributed to simply mathematically defined uniform cycles? *How is the mind of man able to adopt a successful intention to change the course of history from its present trajectory?*

The known features of the demographic characteristics of human populations, as reflected from both history and pre-history, show that the development of the potential relative population-density of the human species is not random in any sense of that term. There is an expressed *intention*, especially in the long-term rise, since the Fifteenth-Century, Italy-centered Renaissance, of the potential relative population-density of globally extended modern European civilization's impact on the demographic characteristics of the human population as a whole.

This factor of intention, corresponding to Kepler's notion of the *Mind* of the planet, is what is expressed, typically, in the form of explicit intention, as those changes associated with the establishment of the modern (e.g., anti-"free trade," anti-"globalization") form of sovereign nation-state economy, and with the correlated emphasis upon both development of basic economic infrastructure, and investment in capital-intensive modes of scientific and technological progress. This accomplishment depends, also, in a more or less crucial degree, on the extent to which a Classical-humanist form of education dominates elementary and secondary education of children and youth.

Thus, although Vernadsky is explicit, in emphasizing the unique quality of noëtic function of mankind, in transforming the biosphere to higher states of anti-entropy, *his argument does not yet define that specific quality of human intention, by means of which that noëtic impulse is expressed as a "trajectory" of such transformation of the biosphere.* This omission is addressed, and corrected, by introducing the *voluntarist* definition of "physical principle" described above. *Here lies our debt to Vernadsky, and, also, the debt of his legacy to us.*

The existence of such a principle, is determined solely by the method identified as, variously, *Analysis Situs,* or *geometry of position.* Recall the three-step process of discovery outlined here earlier.

Given a known, existing array (i.e. *manifold*) of experimentally validated universal principles; given an effect, which that manifold prescribes as necessarily predetermined; and given a description of an experimentally definable effect, the which contradicts, paradoxically, that prescription, that by a significant margin of error. What is the universal principle which must be added to the manifold to bring the manifold into conformity with the thus-expanded view of universal reality? Such a "model" illustrates the general principle associated with geometry of position. Such is the way in which physics, as defined by Riemann's habilitation dissertation, supersedes deductive forms of mathematics in all competent practice of physical science, including the science of physical economy.

The result of such change, as Gauss laid the principal foundations for the discovery featured in Riemann's habilitation dissertation, is a recognition of the experimentally measurable effects of the efficient existence of such principles, in terms of the related change in curvature of the physical space-time defined by the inclusion of the newly discovered principle. Hence, the core argument of Riemann's dissertation. Here lies the essential contribution to all science by Riemann; here lies Riemann's indispensable contribution to the fuller comprehension of the nature of the Keplerian orbits and the deeper implications of the work of Leibniz and Gauss.

How, then, can such an experimentally validated discovery of such a physical principle, be applied willfully to produce a new quality of behavior of the observed manifold considered as a whole?

Exactly the same principle of geometry of position, is expressed by J. S. Bach's discovery of a well-tempered system of tuning, and of his method of counterpoint, inversion, based upon a musical expression of the same principle of geometry of position employed by Fermat for the discovery of a principle of quickest time. Bach's use of inversion, whose lawful ordering is reflected characteristically by the *Lydian principle* celebrated in Beethoven's Opus 132, is a perfect example of the principle of *Analysis Situs,* and of the manner in which that principle generates, in this case for music, a principled notion of musical idea. This is the notion of musical ideas, based on the work of Bach, which defines the absolute separation of the methods of Classical thorough-composition of Haydn, Mozart, Beethoven, Schubert, Mendelssohn, Schumann, and Brahms, from the irrational sensationalism of such Romantics as the silly Rameau, Liszt, Berlioz, and Wagner.

Fermat's argument for a principle of quickest time, in refraction of light, typifies such a paradox of universal import. Kepler's appreciation of the paradoxical implication of the Mars orbit's elliptical form, is also such a paradox. The statement of such paradoxes in the form of contradictions within the manifold of reference in which they erupt, is the conceptual prototype of what is representable by the method of *Analysis Situs* or *geometry of position*.

If the proposed *hypothetical* solution, the new universal principle, is demonstrated, by appropriate form of experiment, to be valid *universally*, that principle is to be added to the manifold. *It is the willful application of such a newly discovered principle of nature, to nature, which causes the relevant change within the manifold as previous extant.* It is the resulting transformation of the manifold, by deleting false assumptions, and adding needed principles, on which the Leibniz notion of characteristic action (i.e., least action) is premised. This notion is already implicit in Kepler's original development of modern astrophysics, and in Leibniz's undertaking the corresponding challenge which Kepler bequeathed "to future mathematicians."

It is the willful action of the individual human mind, in making such a valid discovery of *a pre-existing universal principle* in the universe, which, *by willfully applying that same principle, changes the universe from which that discovery has been adduced.* It is as if to say, that *"In the beginning was the Logos…"* This point of principle, already introduced a few pages earlier, has yet much deeper implications, to which I shall come shortly here, in due course.

I must restate this point just made, for both emphasis and clarity.

The characteristic form of action, which distinguishes the human species, from all inferior forms of life, is those discoveries of universal physical and congruent principle, by means of which the quality of man's functional, demographically expressed relationship to the universe as a whole, is raised to a higher level. These discoveries have the effect, of transforming the entire manifold of man's implied knowledge of universal physical principles.

What I have said here, so far, signifies this. It is not so much the individual such discovery, in and of itself, which is characteristic; it is the transformation of the manifold as a whole, from its state prior to the discovery, into its state after the incorporation of the discovery. It is

this transformation of the manifold, which supplies a validated discovery of principle its universal character. It is that change in the universality of the manifold, which is the subject of the characteristic form of human cognitive action. It is that characteristic which defines the role of human noëtic activity in effecting those transformations which elevate man's existence within the biosphere, to man's dominant role in the noösphere.

It is this role of the thus-informed human will, so informed, which is the pivot of our concern in this report as a whole.

Manifolds so expandable are implicitly of the general form of Riemannian manifolds, as typified by Riemann's 1854 habilitation dissertation.

2. There is an hierarchy of three known, respectively distinct types of manifolds which conform to that definition of universal physical principles: a.) The manifold of *non-living processes* in general; b.) The manifold of *living processes* in general; and, c.) The manifold of *cognitive processes*. The general nature of the experimental distinctions, and interrelations among the three classes of manifolds, is that defined, from the standpoint of biogeochemistry, by Vladimir I. Vernadsky. The three, combined as multiply-connected, constitute what Vernadsky terms a *noösphere*.

Look briefly at these distinctions, using the standpoint set forth by Vernadsky.

There are several types of evidence to be considered as either crucial, or relatively so, in distinguishing life as a universal physical principle, from those notions of universal physical principle associated with non-living processes. In other words, what is the evidence, in support of Vernadsky's insistence, that that living processes are not derived, by "spontaneous" evolution, from non-living ones.

In each case, as with Louis Pasteur's empirical distinction, in chemistry, between non-living and living processes, or Vernadsky's biogeochemical strategy for dealing with this, we are focussing upon an effect which itself is subject to chemical study after the fact, but which is produced, to be a fact, by a living process, that in a way which can not be duplicated "spontaneously" ("objectively") by a non-living one. Look for the most significant of the fine distinctions presented by such cases.

Thus, for example, by the standard of relative weight of the material involved, the Earth's atmosphere and water are composed, predominantly, of non-living processes, but their existence as an atmosphere, oceans, lakes, and streams, is predominantly a product of a living process, the biosphere. Similarly, fossil rock formations and soil. The net result is, non-living material produced by living processes, by a principle of life itself. Vernadsky defines such non-living elements of the biosphere as among the *natural products* of the biosphere.

In a parallel case, similarly, the powers of cognition unique to the human individual, act upon the biosphere, to produce effects in the biosphere which could exist as they do, only as products of human cognition. Since all three categories of universal principles are known by their production of physical effects, these effects are each among the *natural products* of the corresponding processes, and each category, non-living, living, and cognitive is a universal *physical* principle.

The indicated classes of evidence are to the effect, that life is a universal *physical* principle, independent of, but multiply-connected with what are adducibly universal physical principles governing ostensibly non-living processes as such. Vernadsky's biogeochemistry makes that point implicitly. Thus, the universe acted upon the non-living processes, to the effect of producing the preconditions for life. *How did the universe know that it should do this?* Ask this specific question of Johannes Kepler, for example. *How did the universe know that it should produce the preconditions for existence of cognitive life within the development of living processes?* Ask Kepler, again.

Broadly, the implication posed by this evidence, of three, demonstrably distinct classes of universal principle, indicates that their multiple connection must be, a single, multiply-connected manifold, comparable, in the history of philosophy, to the Absolute of Plato, which existed "from the beginning." As Vernadsky suspected, without his having studied Riemann's work in terms of primary sources, the physical universe as a whole is of the Riemannian form associated with the connections among the three distinct types of universal physical principle indicated here.

3. My principled contribution, carrying these conceptions to a higher level than specified by Vernadsky, is two-fold: a.) I defined the form of such manifolds conceptually, from the vantage-point of Riemann's work, which, on the presently known record, Vernadsky (1938) recognized as of interest, but, at last known record, did not actually undertake; b.) I defined *the principle of physical-economic anti-entropy*, from which vantage-point the functional character of the noösphere must be defined.

From the considerations summarized up to this point, the notion of anti-entropy must be situated, conceptually, within the framework of the Riemannian overview of those three classes of universal physical principles. The underlying quality of the multiple-connectedness of a universe so defined, is that it is characteristically *anti-entropic*.

The transformations in that entire manifold, brought about through experimentally validated discovery of universal physical principle, which increase man's power in and over nature, per capita and per square kilometer, are the standard for defining anti-entropy as characteristic of the noösphere. This, stated in the terms of a science of physical economy, supplies the notion for, and, also, proves the existence and definition, and the basis for measurement, of anti-entropy.

4. Each of these three types, when viewed from the standpoint of my indicated, original contribution to this field, is defined as a distinct quality of manifold from the standpoint of those experimental methods appropriate for defining a valid universal physical principle, and yet each successive such manifold, *produces measurable physical effects which can not be generated from within the confines of the relatively lower-order manifold*. As a matter of experimental method, the evidence of this limitation of the relative lower manifold, as Vernadsky points to that principled method, is what supplies the proof that the relatively higher manifold is a form of existence, absolutely differing in both origin and quality from the relatively lower one.

Again, as I have summarized this above: Vernadsky shows the general nature of this proof, for life, relative to non-living processes, and for the noösphere, relative to the subsumed biosphere. The definition of the explicit role of the cognitive processes in determining the change in relative physical-economic anti-entropy of the noösphere, is uniquely my own contribution, a contribution for which I was, originally, chiefly indebted to my adolescent study and defense of Leibniz's notion of a *monadology* (then, as a defense against Kant's *Critiques*).

This form, in which life and cognition effect qualitative changes in the manifold of an otherwise ostensibly non-living universe, is expressed in the transformation of the functional ordering of relations in the relatively inferior domain, by intervention through action from the relatively higher domain. Thus, *as Vernadsky shows, the principle of life, transforms the characteristics of action within the relevant non-living domain, thus defining the biosphere; whereas, as Vernadsky also shows, cognition's intervention transforms the characteristics of action within the manifold of the biosphere. The characteristic of both transformations, is anti-entropy.* Anti-entropy, not the entropy worshipped by the dupes of such Newton devotees as Clausius and Kelvin, is the expression of the highest determining principle of lawfulness in the universe as a whole.

My contribution, on that specific point, has been, chiefly, to define the physical-economic standard by which anti-entropy in the noösphere is to be defined. It is my work to this effect which has made feasible the kind of method required to conquer a crisis of the type immediately threatening civilization today. Vernadsky points to the crucial, anti-entropic role of cognition as such. I shift the center of the focus to the internal functions of the human will, in willfully ordering the direction of the changes in the biosphere brought about through human cognitive intervention.

Since, in all of these exemplary cases, the form of the action is to impose a physical intention upon the universe, or what Kepler would refer to as the intention of the *Mind* of the universe, *any experimentally demonstrated universal principle, is a physical principle in its effects.* Thus, the universal principles attributable to non-living, living, and cognitive processes as such, are each equally universal *physical* principles.

On this account, from the indicated Riemannian view of the implications of the multiple-connectedness of the three specific classes of universal physical principles, the following issues are begged, and also, implicitly, answered in a provisional way.

Vernadsky's argument, as summarized in the referenced, 1938 location, signifies that the universe is a multiply-connected function of three specific classes of universal principles, each distinct from other, yet, because they are always efficiently multiply-connected, each and all subsumed by the correspondingly implied, single universal principle. This multiple-connectedness of that single, underlying principle, as I have just summarized the functional implications of that, above, demands that we recognize the universe as the expression of a single principle of universal creation, whose existence, not "Euclidean" calendars, dates an implied "beginning." *The beginning exists for our knowledge of existence of a self-developing universe, solely as certainty of the existence of a universe which which is universally bounded by itself: a simultaneity of eternity,* within which sequences are ordered by action, not clock-time. Time is determined by cognitively-defined sequences, not sequences by clock-time.

However, it also prescribes, without any possibility of legitimate disagreement, that if one accepts the notion of that principle, the "beginning" is not to be found in the purely fantastic expanses of sense-certainty's pathetic notion of infinitely extended linear time, but rather, as the allegory of Plato's Cave requires, in the real universe, known explicitly only to cognition. It is only in the physical space-time specific to cognition, rather than bestially naive sense-certainty, that the term "beginning," can be used by sane persons, as it is in the opening of the Gospel of St. John.

When those implications are taken into account, we require a correspondingly appropriate definition of the word *creation.* To the degree that mankind discovers those intentions of the Creator's will which are integral to the universality of creation, man takes unto himself, and to his will, the power to employ those intentions, otherwise knowable as universal physical principles, to change the universe in a manner cohering with the principle of universal creation. This, in other words, is man guided by, and acting according to those qualities of *reason* which history shows us are specific to the Classical modes of scientific and artistic discovery and composition.

The power to discover the efficient will to act according to reason so defined, lies in the ability of the individual to rise above the prison-shackles of control by immediate pleasure-pain, to see one's mortal existence as an instrument acting within, and for, the furtherance of that intention which reason unveils to us as the intention (i.e., universal principles) of creation as a whole. Thus, the immediate intimation of immortality is typified by the continuing contributions of valid discoveries of principle supplied to humanity by great scientific minds and great composers of Classical art-forms from centuries and longer before our time.

Enter Monadology As Such

What I have just summarized in the foregoing arguments, should be readily recognized as a restatement, in the context of the most general implications of relevant and crucial qualities of modern discoveries since, of the notion of a *monadology* which Leibniz introduced in a number of locations, chiefly among those specifically addressing that named topic. This must seem less surprising to anyone who takes into account, that I was converted to Leibniz's view on this matter during my adolescent wrestling against the arguments of Immanuel Kant's so-called *Critiques*, as, a decade later, against the degenerate expression of Kant's essential argument by Bertrand Russell and such among Russell's satanic acolytes as Professor Norbert Wiener and John von Neumann.

Now, look again at the relationship between Kepler's definition of the intention expressed by planetary orbits, and the emergence of Riemann's apprehension of the intention of Leibniz's notion of the monad. Situate thus, the choice of approach to be taken to the practical employment of the concept of a monadology.

There are two points of reference, both for defining the notion of characteristics, and for presenting the notion of the *monad* in a fresh, modern way. The one is Kepler's notion of the harmonically ordered, characteristic orbit of each planet, as defined by the Solar System as a whole. The second is the notion of sovereignty, as adduced from the characteristic of the cognitive activity of the individual human mind: Kepler's use of *Mind*, in defining the notion of the *intention* governing a planet's orbit.

The notion of a Keplerian orbit, locates the intention of the orbit in the effect of the position it must *intend* to achieve through motion, as opposed to a position determined by a "Euclidean" form, as a predicate of a mathematically determined trajectory. For Kepler, the relative harmonic value of the orbit, as associated with the equal-areas principle, expressed the nature of this *intention.* The harmonic composition of the orbital composition of the Solar system as a whole, is the second degree of approximation of the *intended* objective of the planet.

This *intention,* expressed by a corresponding *characteristic,* defines a *monad*. The types of existing monads, are assorted among four classes, classes: *non-living, living, cognitive, and absolute*. By "absolute," we should signify "the universe," as a universal simultaneity of the eternity of *ideas*, in which time exists only in the sense of a sequence of actions of a cognitive form. I intend, such a universe, conceived as a monad.

The same principle of the monad, is characteristic of the method of well-tempered composition of J. S.Bach, the method upon which the development of Classical thorough-composition, and related principles of performance, were developed by Haydn, Mozart, Beethoven, Schubert, Mendelssohn, Schumann, Brahms, et al.[32] The "germ form," the crucial contrapuntal inversion on which the entire composition pivots, is associated in *the expressed intention of the composer*, and of the adequate performers, as the anticipated unfolding of the completed composition as to be heard.

The form of Classical musical thorough-composition, which Haydn, Mozart, Beethoven, et al., adduced from the preceding discoveries and their development by J. S. Bach, has the essential quality of reducing the entire composition to a single idea, conceived within the cognitive processes of the mind, the conductor, and so forth, as a single, as-if-instantaneous *idea*: a monad. It is that idea. implying the subsequent unfolding of the entire composition, which underlies, governs the competent performer's attack upon the first note. The performer who fails to attack the opening interval of the composition in that way, will, therefore, fail to communicate *effectively,* the *idea* of the composition as a whole to the relevant audience. This also applies to dramas such as Shakespeare's **Hamlet**, in which a failed choice of attack on "To be, or, not to be," will ensure the failure of the performance of that play from that point through the final, ironical exchange between Fortinbras and Horatio, as the body of Hamlet is carried off stage.

Pause for a moment at this point. From this line of development, Kepler specified the necessary previous existence of a disintegrated planet whose orbit had lain, in a harmonically determined orbit, between the orbits of Mars and Jupiter. About two centuries later, Gauss

---

32. In the case of Brahms, the perfected exposition of that principle is presented in his fourth symphony, which pivots on the quotation of an inversion from the Adagio Sostenuto of Beethoven's "Hammerklavier" sonata, Op. 106. The performances of this directed by Wilhelm Furtwängler are of special importance, because of the latter's reliance on that notion of "performing between the notes" which is integral to the competent performance of a work of Classical thorough-composition, especially a long work as thorough-composed in quality as that Brahms symphony.

LaRouche defines the scientific basis for the application of the voluntarist method of making history, from the vantage-point of earlier breakthroughs, notably the work of Leibniz (left) and Vernadsky (right).

ies of all kinds of universal physical principles, including those of Classical artistic composition.

In the case of Classical irony, such as metaphor or a statement in the form of *Analysis Situs,* the cognitive action "synthesizing" the solution for that paradox, occurs within the sensorially opaque boundaries of the sovereign cognitive processes of the individual thinker. Nonetheless, the ability to demonstrate the truthfulness of the synthesized hypothetical idea, is verifiable by the standards of *unique experimental demonstration*; and the experience of that synthetic act of cognition can be communicated, by replication, within the sovereign cognitive processes of another individual.

The effectiveness of that discovery, expressed as applied to practice, shows both the reality of the idea, and the way in which that idea, although invisible to sense-certainty, can be known efficiently, and that knowledge efficiently shared among persons. This is more readily clear for the case of discoveries in experimental physical science, but it is also that quality of Classical artistic composition which distinguishes it, essentially, from the Romantics and such bastard offspring of Romantic licentiousness as modernism and post-modernism.

Furthermore, the ability of the individual to perform such a cognitive action, either as an original discovery, or its replication by another, depends upon the cultivation of those cognitive powers, as in the mode of a Classical humanist education in accumulated such discoveries from previous history.

Compare Classical artistic principles with those of physical science in the following way.

Look at the Leibniz differential calculus from this vantage-point. The differential there is identical, as a character-type, with the distinctive incommensurability of a Keplerian planetary orbit. The differential must be in the mathematical form corresponding to a statement in *Analysis Situs,* as the role of equal-areas and harmonic characteristic points to the origin of the neces-

was to show, that the asteroids were fragments whose orbital characteristics were those attributed to the missing, disintegrated planet by Kepler.[33] The harmonically defined characteristic of the determining orbit of the planet expresses the principle of the Leibnizian monad.

Thus, the planet's orbit, and also the configuration of the Solar system, are incommensurable, but, nonetheless, predetermined trajectories, as the congruence of the orbital characteristic of the missing planet is reflected in the orbital characteristics of the principal asteroids.

We shall return to consider certain functional implications of that, after comparing the apparent sovereignty of the Solar system of planetary orbits, with the sovereignty of the cognitive processes of the individual human mind. Now that we have a general idea of the principles of physical science as such in view, summarize the case for the second type of principles, those typified by both Classical artistic composition, and the study of history and related topics of statecraft from the standpoint of principles and methods of Classical artistic composition. Focus on the matter of the functional relationship of the cognitive processes of the individuals engaged in the discovery and exchange of discover-

---

33. Cf. Jonathan Tennenbaum and Bruce Director, "How Gauss Determined the Orbit of Ceres," *Fidelio*, Summer 1998.

sary paradoxical expression for the orbit as a whole. That differential is the characteristic of the trajectory in question.

The quasi-sovereign quality of the Leibniz differential, in opposition to the linearized form of Euler, Cauchy, et al., points in the direction of the concept of the monad. It is to be conceptualized as an expression of the ontological principle, "nothing is permanent but change," rather than an expression in terms of the reductionists' axiomatically "Euclidean" physical space-time. *The individuality of the element is its sovereign quality, not its likeness to a sensory object.* Hence, the notion of its existence in the form of a monad.

The implicitly task-oriented transmission of such conceptions of physical science, and their technological derivatives, within the functioning of society, defines the subject of both Classical artistic composition, more narrowly, and the Classical study of history and statecraft, more broadly.

The Sovereign Monad

Look again, at Kepler's use of "Mind," in referencing the *intention* expressed by a planetary orbit. Now, first, compare that *Mind* of the planet with the sovereign cognitive powers of the mind of Kepler. Next, from that standpoint, view the *Mind* of the Sun, expressed in terms of the panoply of orbital characteristics of the orbits of the Solar system as a whole. View that *Mind* of the Sun through Kepler's mind.

After that exercise, then regard the function expressed by the intervention of the physical principle of life, into the ordering of the non-living aspects of the universe. Then, view, similarly, the intervention of the cognitive processes into the ordering of the internal processes of the biosphere. After that, then consider these matters in light of the contrary views on thermodynamics, by Clausius, Kelvin, and Grassmann, for example.

At that point, review what has been considered up to this point, by focussing, first, on the subject of the universal physical principles of life and of cognition, and then return to reexamine the matter of universal physical principles of non-living processes. Start with the human mind and its cognitive powers. To measure, we must first know our measuring instrument; we must begin here, because it is here that we have the knowable concept of the existence of a sovereign mind. We must then compare that notion of a sovereign mind, our own, with the intention shown in its relationship to living processes (the biosphere) and to ostensibly non-living processes, such as planetary orbits, too.

Look inside the cognitive processes of your own mind, the mind within whose sovereign confines that act of discovery occurs, through which mankind's power in and over the universe is potentially increased. Focus upon the congruence, as demonstrated experimentally, between Kepler's discovery of the solution for the fallacies of Copernicus's and Tycho Brahe's work, and Gauss's vindication of Kepler's entire system through the crucial experimental case of the Asteroid orbits. Contrast the congruence of that discovery of principle, as by Kepler, with the failures of Copernicus, Brahe, et al., to escape from the illusory domain of pseudo-realities, the neurotic domain of naive intuition, which mistakes sense-certainty for the real universe.

Hence, such cases—and there are many others, of course—lead to the specific quality of notion of *becoming* which is associated with Plato's dialogues. It is through the faculty of cognition, rather than sense-certainty, that we really know the universe; the idea of the universe presented to our mind by cognition, is not a universe of things swimming, as if in Brownian motion, within some infinite Euclidean soup, but, rather, a universe known to us only through those transformations which result in *changes of axiomatic quality* in our way of thinking about, and acting upon the universe. It is those *changes*, defined in cognitive terms, which are the most elementary form of existence of *ideas*.

For sense-certainty, on the simplest level, eggs or chickens are popularly regarded as self-evident objects. Such is the opinion concerning eggs and chickens among roost-robbers such as skunks, foxes, and sundry varieties of ferrets. In contrast, among cognitively matured persons, in science, the existence of eggs expresses an intention embedded in the existence of chickens, and in the case of chickens, the intention of eggs. However, that intention of chickens or their eggs, does not exist independently of the functional character of the situation in which such intentions are expressed.

It is in the discovery of such intentions, as Kepler adduced the principle of intention, as his notion of universal gravitation underlying the orbit of Mars, that real knowledge of the universe lies. However, the intention of Mars can not be defined, except within the universal setting (situation) of the Solar system as a whole. These notions of intention, are to be contrasted with the Aristotelean dogma of those philosophical incompetents who tolerated Claudius Ptolemy's hoax for so long; or the credulous sophomores who swallow the popular fairy-tale, that Copernicus discovered the orbit of the Sun by the Earth; or, Sunday Supplement grubs who write, that modern European culture is "Copernican." Kepler's notion of intention, typifies a universal conception of existence, as really occurring in no other form than an intention underlying a *becoming*.

This connection of an intention to the notion of a becoming, is the underlying principle of Leibniz's discovery of an actual differential and integral calculus, a discovery to which he was led by a challenge bequeathed "to future mathematicians" from Kepler. A specific quality of intention, as associated with a specific quality of becoming, represents a *characteristic*, in Leibniz' and Riemann's sense of such a term. This notion of a characteristic, is, in turn, the context within which the notion of a Leibnizian monadology dwells.

This point ought to be clear, merely from the standpoint of the experience of any person who has actually made, or has, perhaps as a student might, reenacted a valid discovery of universal physical principle. I restate it, in summary, now.

The case of a paradox expressed in the form of *Analysis Situs,* goes to that point. All discoveries occur as the fruit of solutions to paradoxes of an ontological type. The challenge of that paradox provokes an act of conception. It is that act of conception which, if successful, produces the hypothetical form of a solution to such a paradox, which is brought into being within an individual sovereign mind. The experimental demonstration of the validity of that hypothesis, defines a universal physical principle.

Thus, the cognitive process which generates a validated hypotheses of that type, is typical of the appropriate mental image of reality. The image of the cognitive process we have experienced in ourselves, in either discovering a valid universal physical principle, or reenacting such an historical discovery, is the only actually existing, rational notion of the real existence of anything. Only to the degree that our conceptions are reached by that cognitive method of generating notions of principle, can anyone say truthfully that, "I know."

A person may say, "I saw," or "I heard," or "I touched," or "I smelled," on the basis of confidence in the reliability of one's ability to distinguish between actuality and illusion in matters of sense-experience. When such a person substitutes the verb "to know," for "I saw," or, "I heard," that person is, in the usual case, speaking untruthfully. Nonetheless, sometimes, as in the case of the experimental validation of a universal physical principle, one can justly say of relevant sense-experiences, "I know."

For example, a person testifying that "I saw," may be rightly questioned, "How do you know that that is what you saw?" The person who defends his observation with the outburst, "What I see is what I know!" is committing a misstatement. We do not know what we see; we require some cognitive form of corroboration, before sense-experience can be transformed into knowledge.

For example, in the case the witness testifies, "I saw that man" (pointing), it is often proper, and may be necessary, to follow that response with a series of queries on the statement with "How do you know…?" "How do you know you were not mistaken?" Only in the type of case in which the relevant tests have been actually, or implicitly applied, can a person speak honestly of sense-experience as a matter which "I know."

However, although what I have just written, is a true statement as far as it goes, matters are not quite that simple.

The ability to define reality in a knowledgeable way, free of illusory popular sorts of intuitions, lies in the social relations defined by cognition, rather than in hermetical "Robinson Crusoe" models. It is in the replication of valid discoveries of principle, by one mind in relation to another, that the discoverer becomes *self-conscious of his own cognitive processes*, through their reflection, as the generation of the same idea in the mind of others.

In this reciprocal relationship between two thinkers referencing the same subject of practice, the one recognizes the act of cognition in the other, and anticipates the recognition of the corresponding act of cognition in himself. So, in this reciprocally self-conscious way, the action of cognition is made into an *object* of cognition.

This notion of a *cognitive* form of *self-consciousness,* is the foundation of all competent education in physical science, and the essence of Classical artistic composition and performance.

It is in the ability to share that cognitive discovery of universal principle with others, in a task-oriented way, that real knowledge of the physical universe becomes a subject of conscious intention. It is in the distinguishing of one such idea, from others, of the same cognitive origin, that we are able to distinguish one idea from another one, as a form of existence of ideas, as situated within a social process.

This social aspect of the process of accumulating

valid ideas, cognitively, over successive generations, defines what is properly regarded as Classical principles of artistic composition and performance. The validatable principles of Classical artistic composition, also provide the basis for the apprehension of real history and the arts of statecraft. The discovery of the sovereign nation-state, first accomplished during Europe's Fifteenth-Century, Italy-centered Renaissance, is among the most appropriate examples of this relationship between valid methods of Classical artistic composition, as by Leonardo da Vinci and Rafael Sanzio, and statecraft.

For example, a Classical tragedy, such as that of Shakespeare or Schiller, is based on a problem defined by actual or mythical history (such as the Homeric epics) of an historically specific actual setting.[34] Usually, the composition is true-to-life history. The successfully-performed drama on stage provokes the cognitive processes of the audience into recognizing the implicit error, and probable principled solution to that error, in some calamitous situation in history. The application of the critical (cognitive) faculties, to the business of verifying the appropriateness of the dramatic performance, has, then, the function of an experimental test of an hypothesis; if the critical treatment shows the conception generated to be truthful with respect to the principle of actual history so represented, the drama has performed the function of inducing knowledge in the audience, knowledge in the same sense as a validation, in the laboratory, of the claimed discovery of universal physical principle.

Thus, man's mastery of nature, through the progress of physical science, depends upon man's mastery of the development of the social processes within which the unfolding of history and the practice of statecraft are situated. That is the meaning of Classical science, and Classical artistic composition, as expressed, for example, by the 1776 U.S. Declaration of Independence and the 1789 Preamble of the U.S. Federal Constitution.

The quality which separates Classical from Romantic and other vulgar art, is the difference in the quality of emotion which is essential, respectively, to each. In vulgar art, the relevant emotion is, predominantly, sensual effects. In Classical art, it is the cognitive sensation

of a "light turning on in the mind." So, in the Passions of J. S. Bach, Christ's Gethsemane decision, is the pivotal feature. In the ***St. John Passion***, Bach underscores this by the musical apposition of the hateful cry for Christ's Crucifixion. In the famous Negro Spiritual, "He never said a mumblin' word," it is that "light turning on in the mind" which is the typical referent, in Classical art, for the use of "light," whether in word, or painting. As in Shakespeare's ***Othello***, *There is light, and, then, there is light.*

That "light" of the act of cognitive discovery, or of recognition, is a special quality of passion. That passion is the quality of *movement* in Classical art, and in physical science. This quality of passion, associated with cognitive, rather than deductive-reductionist thinking, is the basis for the emotions described, in thinking about man's physical relationships to the universe, as *motion* and *force* in the universe. In all Classical artistic composition and related thought, this is apprehended as Classical inspiration, and, as the quality of Classical-artistic *action*.[35] These notions of *inspiration for action*, are the basis for the idea of intention, as Kepler employs precisely that method of *Analysis Situs* which I have repeatedly referenced here, to focus his own mind's cognitive powers on the matter of intention in the behavior of the orbiting planet and its Solar system.

The "sense-organ," with which the sovereign powers of the individual mind perceive the manifestation of principle in that physical universe within which the individual person exists, is the "organ" of sovereign powers of the individual's cognition. Just as we represent the sense-experience of sight or hearing with the organ by means of which such perceptions are made, we know the manifestations of principle with a differ-

<hr>

34. The case of the work of Schliemann's physical proof of such ostensibly mythical matters as the matter of the Iliad's site of ancient Troy, is of this type.

35. Here lies the essence of the difference between the Romantic methods, of both composition and performance, of Rameau, Liszt, Berlioz, Wagner, et al., and the Classical methods of composition and performance of Bach, Haydn, Mozart, Beethoven, Schubert, Mendelssohn, Schumann, and Brahms. This is underscored by the way in which that young pupil of the Romantic Czerny, Franz Liszt, went on to attempt, as shown by Liszt's performance transcriptions, even to turn Classical compositions such as Schubert's ***Wanderer*** Fantasy into Romantic slush. In Classical musical compositions, and their performances, it is the resolution, as of Classical metaphor, of what appear to be contrapuntal dissonances, created by Bachian inversion, which is the distinction quality of passion in such music. Furtwängler's "playing between the notes," typifies the method of performance, as opposed to Romantic score-reading for sensual effects, consistent with the Classical world-outlook.

ent kind of "sense-organ," that of cognition. So, the images of universal physical principle are crafted by the mind according to the requirements of the organ through which such qualities of principle are perceived: the organ of sovereign powers of cognition.

So, for cognition of principle, the notions of "light," "inspiration for action," and "sense of motion," are the qualities expressed by our power to sense the actual universe which has prompted the mere shadows on the dimly-lit cavern wall of sense-perception.

These cognitive experiences have also the quality of willfulness, as contrasted with simple passions of the flesh. It is the sense of the way in which universal physical principle embodies a willful intention, such as that of the orbit of Mars, or the principle of universal gravitation as adduced, originally, by Kepler, which is the essence of scientific thought respecting nature outside man. It is the perception of Classical-artistic forms of discovery and expression of universal principle, which lends the intention and capacity of action given to it by inspiration, which imparts to audiences for that art the will to act in concert for the sake of the good.

So-called abstract, "objective," logical thinking, is the intellectual cosmetician's preparation of the departed for its journey into that mass grave where hoaxster Claudius Ptolemy's astronomy, and many other useless fabrications of the pedant are buried. Without cognitive passion, there is no validatable discovery of universal principle, but only the tomb where Kantians and their like are buried, dwelling in Purgatory, because Hell will not receive the doubly dead.

Like that celebrated calculus-faker, Leibniz-hater Leonhard Euler, and Laplace's protege and plagiarist Cauchy after him, Clausius, Kelvin, and Grassmann, among relevant others, concocted what became known as three laws of thermodynamics, on the basis of the purely arbitrary, "ivory tower" assumption, that the universe is implicitly the universe of non-living processes as conceived, axiomatically, by the empiricists and their offspring the positivists.

The later, more radical version of the mid-Nineteenth-Century dogma of Clausius, et al., underwent a further moral and intellectual degeneration, into the forms of radical positivism associated with Bertrand Russell and Ernst Mach. Ludwig Boltzmann come to play a leading role in systematizing the dogma of Clausius et al. Russell acolytes Norbert Wiener and John von Neumann, compensated for their expulsion, for in-

competence and related offenses, from Hilbert's Göttingen University, by concocting the pseudo-scientific dogmas of "information theory" and "systems analysis," and Boltzmann follower Erwin Schrödinger attempted to degrade the discoveries of Pasteur, Vernadsky, et al.,into a dogma not inconsistent with the statistical thermodynamics of Boltzmann.

Thus, today, we have the spectacle of what might be escapees from Jonathan Swift's legendary island of Laputa, promising to create an "artificial intelligence," to replace the human intelligence they have repudiated, and to go to the edge of repudiating life itself, thus to make room on Earth for a proposed proliferation of super-human robots.

With the presently ongoing, epoch-making collapse of the so-called "new economy" based upon such drivel as that of Clausius and his successors, religious adoration of those existentialist Nietzschean supermen called "intelligent robots," will dwindle to the ranks of scattered, Flagellant-like, pathetic bands, as the harsh reality of a need for human intelligence in producing the necessaries of life, will become, once again, predominant.

When we examine the doctrine of Clausius et al., from the vantage-point of considering the axiomatic considerations pervading this present report, that Tower of Babel created by the empiricists and their followers, such as Euler, Laplace, Cauchy, and Clausius, is a self-evident absurdity. These ostensibly human beings assert, as their fundamental, axiomatic assumption, that the universe is created in its entirety, according to a mechanistic sort of implied deductive-reductionist assumption, that "we have yet to discover whether this universe, will or will not, tolerate the existence of life in general, and human life in particular." On recognition of that devastating axiomatic fallacy underlying their entire system of argument, the fallacy of the doctrine of universal entropy should be obvious to all intelligent and reasonably literate adults.

Take the tack opposite to the axiomatic assumptions of those unfortunates. Ask, not whether life is possible, but, rather, what is the nature of the universe, that it brought us into being, and gave us the ability to increase our powers in and over that universe? The argument, expressed as biogeochemistry, by Vernadsky, indicates the direction of the answer to that question which we must ask of ourselves. My own discoveries and related developments in the field of physical economy, enable us today to express what is otherwise implicit in Vernadsky's work, as a basis for shaping policy in and among nations.

The lesser crime of folk such as Euler, Laplace, Cauchy, and Clausius, which is to say, overlooking the evidence of their malicious intentions, is that their focus upon a radical reductionist's deductive scheme for non-living processes, defiantly ignores the Kepler-Leibniz principle of situation (i.e., *Analysis Situs*). They deny, rather hysterically, the universe within which they themselves exist.

Each orbit of the Solar system within which they exist, has a characteristic, expressed as the notion of an incommensurable number. So, each object of scientific inquiry, is defined by a similar type of characteristic, and thus represents a monad in Leibniz's sense of the term. However, these types of characteristics, although they can be distinguished experimentally, do not have precisely the same value in all situations in which they occur. In practice, the value of their characteristic is adjusted to conform to the *situation/position* in which they lie.

This implies, first, a unique number for the object as such, but, also, a uniquely qualified number locating the existence of that numbered monad within the functional context of its *situation/position*.

Thus, entropy exists as an observed phenomenon within the situation in which it appears. Thus, for Pasteur, Vernadsky, et al., ostensibly inorganic matter behaves differently, as such matter, within a living process as its situation, than in a non-living situation of reference, such as a decaying remain of a living organism, or simply in a situation which is immediately a non-living one. Yet, Vernadsky emphasizes, from the standpoint of biogeochemistry, those natural products of the biosphere which appear as typically non-living material, have an "historic" determination within the development of the biosphere, which is their relevant "historical" situation. Here the folly of Clausius and the dupes who follow him, becomes obvious.

This principle of situation, as I have just referenced it, once again, here, is crucial. The general view to be emphasized, even for laymen generally, is the efficiency with which cognitive processes change the characteristics of the biosphere, and in which living processes (e.g., the biosphere) transform the characteristics of non-living ones, that as Pasteur, Vernadsky, et al., have shown.

3. Physical Economy & Life

To go beyond Vernadsky's mapping of the challenge, to the manner in which mankind may willfully change its ostensible present destiny, we have three interdependent categories to add to Vernadsky's 1938 image of the noösphere.

First, basic economic infrastructure. How must we make the desert bloom? What must we do, beyond the preceding beneficial conditions for human life already provided by the biosphere, to bring the biosphere itself to that higher state of organization required to increase mankind's power to exist in and over the universe? On this point, our argument directly overlaps that of Vernadsky.

Second, the development of those processes of production upon which the maintenance and improvement of human existence at present and improved levels depend.

Third, the constitution of the organization of society, and of the education and general culture of its people, that in ways which make possible the cooperative efforts required to organize society's efforts in ways which are appropriate, for both the needed improvements in basic economic infrastructure, and processes of physical production and distribution of essential goods and services.

The three are suitably combined as a single topic, under the heading of the self-improvement of the reproduction of the demographic characteristics of the human species and its households. The principal measurements are made *per capita* and *per square kilometer* of the normalized cross-section of the biosphere. It is the rate of improvement of those characteristics, which is the focus of measurement of estimated values: i.e., *rate of rate of change* of such values.

I begin by focusing upon the role of basic economic infrastructure as the leading feature of the interface between the noösphere and biosphere. On this point, I include some restatements of what I have stated in locations published earlier.

What Is Basic Economic Infrastructure?

Generically, the term "basic economic infrastructure" should be employed to signify all those improvements in the whole land-area, as land-area, which are required to create the preconditions under which "the desert may bloom." This includes the general development of *transportation, water-man-agement,* and *power systems.* This also includes emphasis on the *development and management of field and forest in ways which increase the rate of conversion of solar radiation into forms of biomass usable in ways which are to the benefit of promoting the maintenance and increase of the productive powers of labor.* Thus, *it includes urban planning and development, in addition to managed fields and managed forests.*

Look at this in the terms Vernadsky defines the relationship between biosphere and noösphere. Now define that relationship in functional terms, first from Vernadsky's standpoint, and, after that, the standpoint of the science of physical economy.

The geological "history" of the

Magnetic levitation trains anchoring development corridors across continental Eurasia would more than pay for the cost of building and maintaining such corridors, by increasing the production of physical goods. The Shanghai maglev, shown here at the Long Yang Road Station.

Earth, as portrayed from the standpoint of biogeochemistry, indicates that the pattern of apparent evolutionary emergence of species, must focus less on the idea of evolution by species, and more on the way in which the self-development of the biosphere, through accumulation of its natural products (such as atmosphere and oceans), *creates the preconditions on which the emergence of higher types of species depends.* The significance of the emergent species then becomes, primarily, the impact of its existence in changing the characteristics of the biosphere as a whole manifold.

This self-development of the biosphere, as a biosphere-process, came to the point, some unknown quantity of millions of years ago, at which *conditions of the biosphere necessary for the cognitive life-form, man, were sustainable.* Into this image, we must inject the notion of mankind's further transformation of the biosphere, as through what Vernadsky implicitly defines as the *natural products* of noetic (human) life, including cultivated forms of fields and forests, and what we today must recognize as the forerunners of modern basic economic infrastructure.

Suppose, then, that society operates to the effect, that a minority of the total population enjoys the benefits of infrastructural improvements, while the majority does not. Then, the development of the potential productivity of the majority will be crippled. We shall soon return, here, under the heading of the nation-state, to

that crucial consideration.

Look at central Asia today. There are vast areas with abundance of what are called "natural resources," but which are condemned, so far, to be greatly underdeveloped, for lack of the basic economic infrastructure. There, a dense, highly productive population might live. To bring that change about, basic economic infrastructure must be developed to the point that development corridors combining mass transportation, large-scale water-management, and generation and distribution of power, were supplied within development corridors of up to 100 kilometers width. Such a network of emerging corridors would transform much of this sparsely developed region into a rich potential for growth of population and its prosperity.[36]

Moreover, with high-speed (e.g., magnetic levitation) transport of freight across continental Eurasia, from locations such as Rotterdam into Japan, and across the Bering Straits, the efficiency of investment in development of physical production of goods would be greatly increased over the present degree of reliance upon transoceanic freight. Every mile (or, kilometer) of such development corridors more than pays for the cost

36. On the European Productive Triangle, see footnote 4. On the Eurasian Land-Bridge, see Jonathan Tennenbaum et al., ***The Eurasian Land-Bridge: The 'New Silk Road'—Locomotive for Worldwide Economic Development*** (Washington, D.C.: EIR News Service, Inc., January 1997).

of building and maintaining such development corridors, a more-than-compensating income experienced in the form of production occurring along each 50 miles or so of the route. This is contrasted with the general lack of production across most of each 50 miles of a transoceanic transport. In that sense, because of the increased output and increased productivity it makes possible, a well-developed, and properly explored development corridor, costs the economy much less than a net nothing.

Thus, we must recognize that the superimposition of the noösphere upon the pre-noösphere condition of the biosphere, is not merely something slapped down on top of that biosphere, but, instead, signifies an acceleration of the development within the biosphere as a biosphere, *to the intended effect* of enhancing the preconditions for human development, while also increasing the rate of functional throughput of a biosphere which now includes man and man's activities as part of that biosphere.

I would emphasize the attention of space-scientist Krafft Ehricke to the "industrialization of the Moon," and my extrapolation of that policy, to generating the synthesized natural biospherical-like conditions for a Los Alamos-scale of laboratory-station on Mars. To restate the point: the Solar system developed the preconditions for a biosphere's self-development on Earth, in the course of which, the preconditions for human life emerged. In long-term space-exploration, in which men and women stay "in space" for months or longer, we can not rely indefinitely upon so-called "artificial life support." We must utilize the principles of the biosphere, as we learn those lessons from the emergence and maintenance of human life on Earth, to assist us, increasingly, in developing replications of biosphere-like processes "in space."

Therefore, the development of the biosphere was continued, chiefly through what I have described here as basic economic infrastructure, as an integral part of a noösphere which subsumed it. Our continuation of that process of development of the biosphere (under the reign of the noösphere) is a precondition for the emergence of higher levels of human existence. Man, thus, raises the level of development of the biosphere above that achieved by the pre-human biosphere.

Now, thus, the natural products of a biosphere situated within a noösphere, aggregate to a higher level of quality and relative mass than under the "natural" state which might be achieved by the biosphere alone. For example, man-managed forests, if properly managed, are far less prone to devastating forest fires than the forests of an untamed wilderness. For example, the managed distribution and reprocessing of water, makes possible a great increase of the quantity and quality of biomass per square kilometer. For example, looting family farms down to the bone, with Carter-administration-level sub-parity prices paid directly to farmers, turns vast tracts of agricultural and related land-area into dust-bowls, as occurred in the U.S.A. over the 1920s and early 1930s.

Just as the principle of life intervenes into non-living processes, to change the latter's behavior to the effect we may recognize as the biosphere, so man's cognitive intervention into the development of the biosphere, alters the behavior of the biosphere. In such cases, the subsumed domain's internal laws of behavior of the subject-matter are altered, to the effect Pasteur and others noted in the cases of the fermentation of beer and wine. These changes are measurable, as natural products of life. So, cognition's intervention into the biosphere, redefines biosphere as including those categories of behavior which we recognize as basic economic infrastructure. These changes in the biosphere are measurable ones, and are the preconditions for the maintenance and improvement of human life. They are natural products of the noösphere, and must be so recognized and assessed.

The measurement required, by a science of physical economy, is the *relative rate of increase of the potential population-density of the human population,* taking into account associated improvements in life-expectancy, and improvements in the demographic characteristics of both households and the population in general, their general welfare, as the U.S. Constitution's Preamble specifies that goal to be the inalterable law governing the decisions of our republic.

Production As Such

The standard for measure of productivity is not counted output as such, but, rather, the *relative* rate of increase, stagnation, or decline of the productive powers of labor. This measurement is made in both per-capita and per-square-kilometer terms, and is qualified by the requirement of improvements in the demographic characteristics of family households, and of the population in general. These measurements approximate, and express in that degree, the notion of relative potential population-density. In other words, these are different ways of measuring with fair approximation, the rates of change in the anti-entropy of what Vernadsky defined as the noösphere.

At this point, it is important to forewarn those critics, once more, who might demand a mathematically exact standard of measurement. All important constants in physical science are, by their nature, relative values, and thus ultimately incommensurable. In the topical area of national and world economy, we would warn critics that the value of production, and productivity, considered in the small, varies according to the characteristics of the so-called macro-economic setting in which it is situated. The point of using approximations, is not that our measurements are not sufficiently refined in detail; the point is, that any changes in the noösphere in which the economy is situated, alters the functional value to be assigned implicitly to any localized subject-matter.

Take a case from physics in general. There are strong experimental indications, from work conducted by scientists over decades, that what are usually considered universal constants, may not be exactly constant, but may be altered by the impact of radiation from stellar space, and, at least under certain conditions, may be different for materials subsumed within living processes than is to be found among the same species of monad found in non-living processes. Thus, in physical science generally, and in economics more narrowly, we must think of characteristics as being incommensurables in the final analysis, as Kepler did.

The magnitude, the characteristic, we are attempting to measure, at least in a reasonable degree of approximation, is a true characteristic, unique to the orbit or other monad-like existence to which it refers. But, we must never forget, that the universe is not the sum of its parts, but a manifold, which is the context and determinant for the existence of each part. Valid new discoveries will not make a characteristic less characteristic; but the exact number associated with it is never known in the nth degree, and may be subject to some significant modification as the extent of our knowledge of the universe is increased.

In changing the biosphere, as the noösphere's existence does, we are changing the "macroscopic" economic manifold within which each act of production, or other economically significant local action occurs. Thus, all estimates of local economic values of production and related things, are approximations. The distinctions made among local such events may be only approximations, but the estimated relative values have the kind of significance for practical application which the idea of a competent approximation suggests.

The paradigmatic essence of the noösphere, is the act of cognition through which the individual mind generates a valid discovery of universal physical principle. Here lies the essence of the quality of anti-entropy specific to the noösphere, the functional distinction of noösphere from biosphere. *Here lies the key to mankind's unique and specific ability to change the universe.*

The construction of the equivalent of what is called, after Riemann, a *unique* experiment, is not only the indispensable proof of a universal physical principle. It is from the requirements of the design of such an experiment, that what we call *technologies* are spun from scientific discoveries of universal principle. One of the most efficient examples of that, is Wilhelm Weber's unique experimental demonstration of the Ampere angular force principle for electrodynamics. The proof of principle is expressed in the design of the experimental apparatus; conversely, it is from examination of the crucial features of the machine-tooled design of the experimental apparatus, that the feasibility of application of the principle flows.

Thus, in modern economy, especially in connection with what are called "crash" science-driver programs, a close, symbiotic kind of reciprocal relationship should exist among the research scientists, the machine-tool-design functions, and the introduction of the validated technology, through highly skilled development teams, into the processes of product-design and production methods. In such cases, the principal variable in net performance, is the development of a corresponding structure of employment of the total labor-force, such that the "science driver" components and the immediately supporting strata, are an increasing ration of the total employed labor-force.

Thus, a willful up-shift in the composition of categories of occupations and employment in the total labor-force, must be a process of bringing an increasing portion of that labor-force in ever-closer proximity to "pure physical-economic" generation of rapid rates of advances in technology of both production and product design. It would be useful to call that *the sociological principle of anti-entropy in the noösphere*. We shall return to some crucial implications of this same point, but from a different vantage-point, at a slightly later point in this concluding section of my present report.

The development of the accumulation of experimentally validated discoveries of universal physical principles, takes the form of a Riemannian manifold. The addition of new such discoveries, results in the establishment of a new manifold. *It is the implicitly measurable anti-entropy generated by such an unfolding series of manifolds, which is crucial.* The advance of the development of this manifold is the underlying characteristic which drives physical-economic progress as such. However, the relative benefits to an economy depend upon the willingness and ability of the society to utilize the benefit of such discoveries in terms of transformations in employment, product-design, production itself, and also the development of basic economic infrastructure in a manner and degree which these up-shifts in the technological potential require for their effective implementation in production and distribution.

For example, on the matter of infrastructure. Take, first, the case of power. The ability to realize the benefits of valid discoveries of universal principle, and of related technologies, generally requires an increase in not only the energy-output per capita and per square kilometer, but also such qualitative improvements as increased energy-flux density, and coherent organization of the energy-flows in distribution and application.

In the case of water management, the amount of water throughput required, per capita and per square kilometer, increases. This requirement can be satisfied only by aid of increasingly sophisticated methods of desalination and reprocessing of water.

In transport of freight, the ability to balance the relationship between inventories of work in progress, and of final product, requires the kind of revolutionary improvements in transportation which builds freight-classification and related matters of delivery and inventory management into the inherent characteristics of the system. The use of magnetic levitation transport for passengers, is impressive; but should not obscure the fact that the potential benefits in terms of freight handling and related matters, are far more impressive economically than faster transport of passengers.

In the notion of urban infrastructure, it should be easily recognized by persons with even ordinary literacy, that the way in which cities have been transformed during the post-World War II period to date, has been increasingly catastrophic in its projectable medium- to long-term effects. The way in which "suburbanism" was pushed, as with New York's Levittown, or the use

of what had been launched, for the nuclear-weapons age, as the national defense highway system, to extract suburbanite ground-rent from former cow-pastures and the like, has been economically, socially, and morally counterproductive, in a very large degree.

Commuters travel further and further. Social life, in the household, and otherwise, deterioriates accordingly. Cities should be built from the subsurface, upward, with principal features of the substructure and other structures intended to remain functional for hundreds of years to come. Given the condition of economic and related rot which has been accumulating inside the U.S.A. and other parts of the world, during, especially, the recent thirty-five-odd years, we are not presently positioned to implement the kind of technological revolution in urban designs to which reason would already point us today. Sometimes, when we have a serious problem, in life, in a nation's economy, we lack the means to make the obvious corrections; but, experience shows, that being aware of the problem, which we might not have the present means to correct entirely, warns us against continuing the undesirable trend, and orients us toward launching the new trends required for the benefit of coming generations, and the national interest, otherwise defined, as a whole.

The Modern Nation-State

The evidence is clear. The greatest rate of improvement of the conditions of life of humanity ever recorded, came as a result of developments within Europe's Fifteenth-Century Renaissance. [**Figure 1**] Through the intertwined role of France's Jeanne d'Arc, the great ecumenical council of Florence, King Louis XI's founding of the first modern sovereign nation-state, and a similar revolutionary role played by Richmond (Henry VII) in England, a new kind of political institution was created in Europe at that time. This was the principle, that *no government has the moral authority to govern, except as it is efficiently committed to promoting the general welfare of all of the population and its posterity.* This led to the later Eighteenth-Century founding of the first true modern sovereign nation-state republic, that of the U.S.A., during the interval 1776-1789. I have addressed this matter, in numerous publications and public addresses delivered over a span of decades. It is necessary to summarize some of that material again, here, in order to make a clear point.

All cultures in known history, prior to that Fifteenth-Century revolution in the practice of statecraft, were

FIGURE 1

Growth of European Population, Population-Density, and Life-Expectancy at Birth, Estimated for 100,000 B.C.–A.D. 1975

Alone among all other species, man's numerical increase is a function of increasing mastery over nature —increase of potential population-density—as reflected historically in the increase of actual population-density. In transforming his conditions of existence, man transforms himself. The transformation of the species itself is reflected in the increase of estimated life-expectancy over mankind's historical span. Such changes are primarily located in, and have accelerated over, the last six-hundred years of man's multi-thousand-year existence. Institutionalization of the conception of man as the living image of God the Creator during the Golden Renaissance, through the Renaissance creation of the sovereign nation-state, is the conceptual origin of the latter expansion of the potential which uniquely makes man what he is.

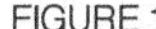

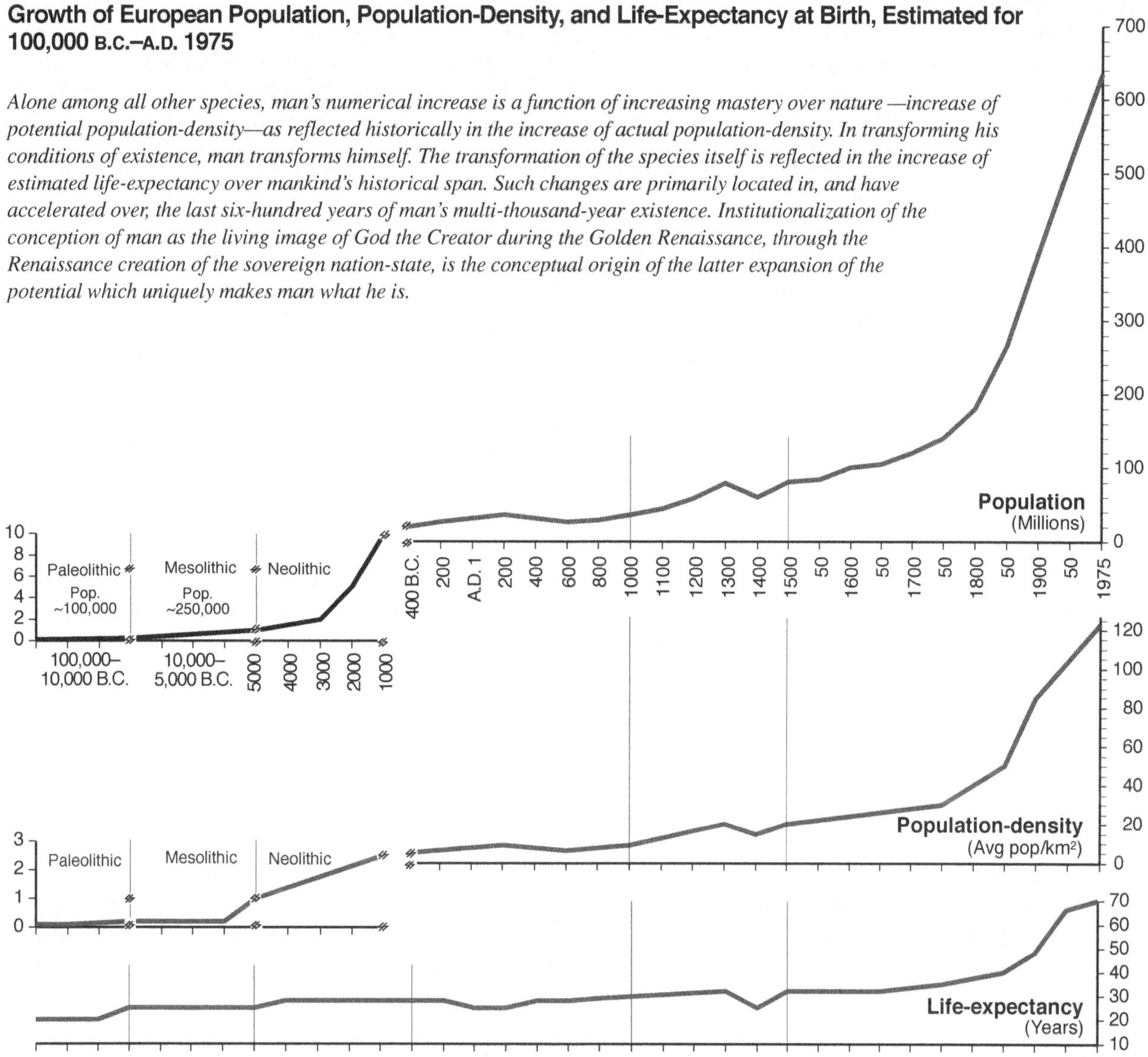

All charts are based on standard estimates compiled by existing schools of demography. None claim any more precision than the indicative; however, the scaling flattens out what might otherwise be locally, or even temporally, significant variation, reducing all thereby to the set of changes which is significant, independant of the quality of estimates and scaling of the graphs. Sources: For population and population-density, Colin McEvedy and Richard Jones, *Atlas of World Population History*; for life-expectancy, various studies in historical demography.

Note breaks and changes in scales.

like the imperial tyrannies spawned in ancient Mesopotamia. They were of a form consistent with what Classical Greek writers knew as the *oligarchical model*. In this general class of types of societies, a relative few, a ruling caste, or oligarchy, aided by a retinue of armed and other lackeys, ruled over the majority of their own and other people, degrading those over whom they ruled to the condition of wild or herded human cattle. The oligarchy variously hunted, herded, bred, and culled those herds, as a farmer takes wild game from the field and forests, and culls his herd of those specimens considered too independent in their impulses, or an excess or otherwise undesirable portion of the total population. Such was ancient Babylon, such was the Sparta designed, like Rome after it, by the Delphi cult of the Pythian Apollo.

This was the condition of mankind under the Roman empire, both in the West and Byzantium. This was the condition, as specified by the Code of the Roman Emperor Diocletian, which became the backbone of what passed for law under European feudalism.

Although the idea of the republic was well defined by Plato, and although the fundamental principle of U.S. constitutional law, the so-called "general welfare"clause, was inherent in Christianity, the struggles to bring about a just society, so constituted, were frustrated until Europe's Fifteenth-Century revolution in statecraft, a revolution summed up by two influential writings of that period, by Nicholas of Cusa: his *Concordancia Catholica*, defining a community of principle among sovereign nation-states, and his *De Docta Ignorantia*, the founding work of modern experimental science. It was Cusa and his immediate circles, who prepared the way for, and inspired, voyages such as that of Christopher Columbus, and launched the evangelization carried into such places as the Americas.

During the interval from the period of the Second and Fourth Crusades, and continuing into late during the Seventeenth Century, Venice emerged as the chief enemy of the attempt to develop the modern nation-state. This was the Venice which had emerged from those crusades as an imperial maritime power, throughout the Mediterranean littoral and Europe generally. In the effort to abort the development of the sovereign nation-state and the new quality of culture it represented, Venice drowned Europe in repeated religious wars over the interval 1511-1648, concluding with the 1618-1648 Thirty Years War.

Under these conditions of the 1511-1648 interval, and still later, more and more of the republican leaders in Europe looked to the Americas as a place to build up colonies which could be developed into sovereign nation-state republics. There were frustrated, if often heroic efforts to that purpose among the independence movements of Central and South America, but only in the United States was a true such republic established. The 1776 Declaration of Independence and 1789 Preamble of the U.S. Federal Constitution typify this connection to the Fifteenth-Century Renaissance.

Ours was an embattled republic from the beginning. With the July 14,1789 storming of the Paris Bastille by those who had been or were the agents of London's Lord Shelburne and Jeremy Bentham, France, the U.S.A.'s chief ally of the 1776-1783 War of Independence, fell into the 1789-1794 Jacobin Terror, and, thence, under the reign of Barras and the first modern fascist, Napoleon Bonaparte.[37] With the outcome of the Congress of Vienna, the U.S.A. was isolated and imperilled, from without (from London and the Holy Alliance) and from the American Tories among financier and slaveholder interests within. Then a great protege of former President John Quincy Adams, President Abraham Lincoln, defeated Britain's Confederacy puppets in the Civil War, and, in concert with Henry C. Carey, launched the great agro-industrial development which established the U.S. economy as the most powerful, and technologically most advanced among nation-states of the world. This established *the American System of political-economy*, of Alexander Hamilton, Mathew Carey, Friedrich List, and Henry C. Carey, as the best form of economic policy existing among the nations of the world.

With the 1901 assassination of President William McKinley, the government of the U.S. fell into the hands associated with two unrepentant heirs of the Confederacy, Presidents Theodore Roosevelt, and overt Ku Klux Klan fanatic Woodrow Wilson. President Coolidge was no better. Under the conditions of a great economic crisis and the onrushing threat of a new world war, President Franklin Roosevelt returned the U.S., for a while, to the American intellectual tradition expressed in its Declaration of Independence and the Preamble of its Federal Constitution. Nixon's Southern Strategy campaign of 1966-1968 marked the turn leading into a return to the reign of neo-Confederacy ideologies and practices of Teddy Roosevelt, Woodrow Wilson, and Coolidge, within the top ranks of both leading political parties.

Throughout its history to date, that American intellectual tradition has been inseparable from an ecumenical foreign policy. It was so with Benjamin Franklin. This was expressed by the 1823 Monroe Doctrine crafted by the Franklin-trained John Quincy Adams; it was the heritage of Abraham Lincoln, and the theme of

---

37. The self-defined "new Caesar," Napoleon was the model copied by Mussolini, Hitler, and other fascists of the post-Versailles decades. The model for modern fascism was prescribed by Bonaparte enthusiast, and sometime Metternich agent, Prussia's state philosopher G.W.F. Hegel. Although Karl Savigny was influenced by and sympathetic to Hegel, the most consistent follower of Hegel was the Carl Schmitt on whose Hegelian doctrine of law, and included theory of the state, the enactment of the decree of February 18,1933, establishing the Nazi dictatorship, was premised.

Franklin Roosevelt's "Good Neighbor" policy and President John F. Kennedy's "Alliance for Progress." Nixon's Secretary of State Henry A. Kissinger typifies those who, out of their own mouths, have been consistently on the opposite side.

That summary overview thus supplied, now focus upon those axiomatic features of the sovereign form of modern nation-state which account for its vast superiority over all earlier cultures in promoting the general welfare of mankind.

The functional distinction of the sovereign form of modern nation-state republic, is that it ends the subjugation of the majority of the population to the status of virtual human cattle. It is the shaping of economic and related policies according to that intention, which imposes upon government the responsibilities for: a.) protecting the national economic development, as measured in per-capita and per square-kilometer terms; b.) the promotion of the development of the basic economic infrastructure of the national territory as a whole; and, c.) the promotion of scientific progress and use of the technologies so derived, to promote the advancement of the productive powers of labor of all of the households of which the population is composed.

It was the approximation of such measures, under Louis XI, which resulted in the virtual doubling of the national income of France under the few decades of his reign. The electrifying transformation of England, under Henry VII, is a comparable case. It was these and related policies, derived from the axiomatic features given authority during the Fifteenth-Century Renaissance, which embedded in the impact of those radiated features of the modern sovereign form of nation-state, the impetus for its unprecedented effect of improving qualitatively the demographic conditions of life of populations.

In all of this, the essential point is, the promotion of the development and application of the individual person's cognitive powers, both in terms of science and technology, and in the cultural activities properly classed under the heading of principles of Classical artistic composition.

As is typical of the way in which the United States has been self-destroyed under the influence of existentialist degenerates such as Theodor Adorno and Hannah Arendt, the greatest crime which recent decades have perpetrated upon the families of the U.S.A.,

is far less the oppression of their bodies, than the degree of success in destroying their souls. By denying the existence of knowable truth, that in favor of mere opinion, and rejecting the socratic methods by which the individual may discover truth, and by imposing methods of classroom and related education, which emphasize the sensual, as opposed to the cognitive, the mental powers, and morals of the population have been greatly undermined, where they have not been yet destroyed.

It is the florescence of Classical education and practice in science and art, which nourishes what becomes both the productive potential of the population, and its inclination to cooperate in bringing related improvements in the material and cultural conditions of life into general practice. The human individual is naturally creative; that distinguishes him, or her, from the beasts. That is the quality of that individual, which, if evoked and encouraged, is the source of upward tracks of revolutionary improvements in the condition of mankind. That, which Plato and the Apostle Paul would identify as the principle of *agapē*, is the power of mankind to change the universe.

Lyndon LaRouche's university textbook on national economic policy, which also serves as a manual for government officials and advisors to governments.